People, Pets, Poems & Epigrams

Some Things That Come with Life

BOBBY BROWN

People, Pets, Poems & Epigrams

ISBN 978-0-9850544-3-4

Appreciations & Thanks

To my wife, Gail, my editor, best friend, companion in marriage for fifty-four-plus years, and love from the 8th grade and now over sixty-five years in real life. How she has put up with me is a mystery. A so-called writer is a hard person to get along with, particularly when someone wants to correct or rewrite what he thinks is so clever, witty, and smartly phrased. Sometimes the writer is not as smart and clever as he thinks he is, so he needs someone who is smarter in grammar and the structures of the writing world to help keep him from looking like a fool with a pencil. I don't like it sometimes and have to argue about it, but in reality, I could not do without her as either an editor or a wife. How lucky can one man be to have all this wrapped up in a live-in package? This is my third book that she has been in charge of fixing. I hope she will agree to still be married when it is finished.

Thanks to my family members for their contributions. Also, thanks to my friends who served as "advanced critical readers." Their judgments, opinions, and ideas were very important and helpful in making decisions on the content before going to print.

—BB

Dedicated to my children and grandchildren so that they might remember some of my stories and advice being handed down.
—BB

The Writer's Note to the Reader

What I Hope You Get from This Book

When you acquired this book, you got more than just a book of words. You got hundreds of hours of work by the writer that includes correcting errors and written experimentations. You now have the times of frustration that the writer experienced caused by the multitudes of required rewrites and throwaways. You see the writer's tears that were shed on the paper for the moments of sorrow recounted. You can now share with him his laughter over the words of a funny story or saying. You also possess the moments of pure joy when the writer realized in his heart what he had just written was truly worth saving. When you got this book, you got a piece of a heart and soul.

I entitled this book *People, Pets, Poems & Epigrams* because that's just what it is. All one can write about are the things experienced or imagined. I wanted to write about all the above that have made my life so full and enjoyable and, yes, brought moments of true heartbreak. I am pleasured in putting words to paper about happenings and events that have made life what it has been for me.

People/Places: These are firsthand stories of some of the people and places woven with me in this bolt of cloth called life.

They are a part of shaping, directing, and helping me be who I am—some of it good, some not so good. There are people here who just made my life's direction change in one way or another. Others are here just for the fun of the story. Perfection is not the goal, but living this life as full as possible is a goal that most all seek. I can tell you only about mine.

Pets: They come into our lives through our children, our friends, and our own making and help bring out who we really are.

Poems: I have always loved poetry, not all but the ones I could understand. I have included a few of mine, my children's, and my grandchildren's.

Epigrams: One dictionary describes epigrams as short, witty, wise, pleasant, or sarcastic comments with some in poetic form. They lay scattered from the front to the back of this little book.

Sharing Something Learned from a Great Writer

A few years ago, my wife's friend recommended a book. As Gail would read, sometimes she would laugh out loud. "Bob," she said, "you are going to love this book." The author's name was Ferrol Sams. I read it with fascination not only for the story but also for my love of his style of writing. I also read his other books.

Sometime later, we saw Mr. Sams being interviewed on YouTube, and the moderator asked him this question: "Mr. Sams, for whom do you write?"

He thought for a moment and then replied, "I never really thought about it before, but I guess I write for myself."

I learned something very important at that moment: I also write for myself. It is a way of cleansing one's soul, so to speak. I hope those who choose to read what is here will also enjoy just a few of the captured moments in time from these pages.

This is a book you can start reading in the middle, the back or the front and not have to worry about finding your place again. Just open to a page or two and keep reading. You will find within these pages, thirty-five epigrams, twenty-two stories, fourteen poems and some other stuff. Included are subjects that might make you grin, laugh, think and maybe cry a little. You will learn that there are some wonderful folks from North Carolina and "round about."

Happy reading.
Written and compiled by Bobby Brown
Storyteller and Eyewitness
2015

Contents

People, Pets, Poems & Epigrams

To start you thinking, try a few of these epigrams. (Note: I heard it said that for a book to be wildly popular with the readers, it must have something sexy in it. Below in Epigram #1 is my only contribution on that subject to this book.)

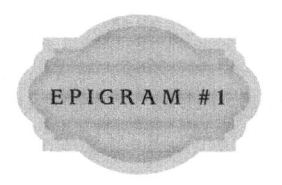

EPIGRAM #1

Learning to Talk Sexy to a Female

As I remember, my first curious sexy line to a female was when I was about seven years old. It went something like this: "I'll show you mine if you will show me yours." It didn't work often, but thank goodness after seventy years I am still interested. I didn't say I still used the line; I just said that I am still interested.

—*BB*

Life's Skateboard

Life is akin to riding a skateboard:
Some people will be going along real fast,
Swerving, jumping, and cutting,
While others, well, they just fall on their asses.
    —BB

On Writing

A good writer can take you to new places you have never been or back to places where you are delighted to return.
    —BB

More On Writing

A friend told me that a student asked his college English professor just how long the essay he was assigned to write should be. The professor replied, "It should liken to a woman's skirt: short enough to be interesting but long enough to cover the subject."

—*Credited to Professor John McLoud and Winston Churchill*

Having Things

Life is not about the things we have. Life is about the memories we make with them.

—*BB*

An Accident At School

A serious accident happened at a local school in a small southern town. Fortune would have it that no one was seriously harmed. An onlooker speaking to no one in particular said, "Why would God let something like this happen in our school?" A young boy, about second- or third-grade age, replied, "They don't allow God in our school anymore."

—*Unknown*

A Question

Are you seventy years old yet? If so, you had better carry a pen and paper.

—*BB*

Liabilities

Your liabilities may be your best assets.
—*BB*

More On Writing

Why is it that most of the really good story ideas come to me at 2:45 in the morning when I am trying to sleep?
—*BB*

On Going to Bed Angry

Married couples should never go to bed angry. Just stay up all night and fight.
—*Unknown*

On Old Hymns

If I make it to heaven, it will not be anything I have done
But will be for the love of old hymns that are very well sung.
 —*BB*

On Writing

It can be said that writing is drawing pictures with words.
 —*BB*

STORY #1

NC People, Places & Other Tales

A Lesson On Life:
You Can't Stay in the Backseat Forever

In one of the comic strips, that great philosopher Charlie Brown once made what I consider a profound observation. Charlie is leaning against a tree talking to Lucy.

She asks, "What do you think security is Charlie Brown?"

He says, "Security is sleeping in the back seat of a car when you are little and you've been somewhere with your mom and dad and it's night. You don't have to worry about anything. Your mom and dad are in the front seat and they're doing all the worrying. They take care of everything."

Lucy smiles and says, "That's real neat Charlie Brown."

Then, he gets a serious look on his face and says, "But it doesn't last. Suddenly you're grown up and it can never be that way again. Suddenly it's all over and you'll never get to sleep in the back seat again. Never!"

Lucy gets a frightened look on her face and asks, "Never?"

And Charlie Brown replies, "Never!"

They stand there, sensing the terrible loneliness that goes with being an adult, and Lucy reaches over and says, "Hold my hand, Charlie Brown."

A sad story here with Charlie and Lucy but a real one. We are not born to stay in the backseat. Charlie has it right. If you stay in the backseat, you miss all the wonderful things that life has to give.

Remember the backseat for the cozy and safe feeling, but do all you can to become the driver and get on down the road of life. You see things a lot better from the front seat.

—BB

EPIGRAM #13

On Speaking

A supposed good friend called me a short time back and said that they were having a company retiree luncheon and had been looking for a well-known, intelligent, and entertaining speaker for the event. He went on to say that "since we haven't been able to find a speaker of that caliber on that date, I thought about you and wondered if you might come and fill in?"

—BB

NC People, Places & Other Tales

A Life-Changing Place: Old Davis Park, Belmont, NC
From a Program Speech by Bobby Brown at the Belmont
Sports Hall of Fame Banquet, November 1999

What I am about to pass on to you is special, and the true fact is there are not many people still alive today who know the things I am about to tell you.

The Belmont Sports Hall of Fame is about remembering people and events, recalling their history, and putting them up front so we can remember them for their achievements.

I would like to step beyond the hall for a few minutes and take us all back a few years to remember something else, back to a place that, for many years, touched the lives of almost everyone in the town in some way.

I hold in my hand a document—a document that is old. This piece of paper represents the foresight of the leaders of this community more than sixty-five years ago. It is the contract for the building of Old Davis Park. This place of magic is named after Mr. W. W. Davis, who owned the land where the park is now built. What a wonderful old place in the community that has touched the lives of thousands of people.

It was started in 1936, right in the middle of the Great Depression. It was completed in 1937 for the grand price of

$28,244.77. This ballpark was built for the people. Some said, at the time, it was the finest baseball field between Washington, D.C., and Miami, Florida.

In 1937, the fans saw the first American Legion National Regional played at the park. The 4,000-seat stadium overflowed. In 1938, the Legion National Regional Playoffs were again staged here at Davis Park. American Legion Baseball teams were brought in to Belmont by train from Maryland, Washington, and Virginia. Our own area was being proudly represented by Gastonia. Eighteen hundred more bleacher seats were brought in and set up down each foul line to accommodate over 7,000 fans gathered from all over for this tournament.

For the price of thirty-five cents, you could get a general admission ticket or pay one dollar for the whole series.

After the war, the old Belmont Combers was the semi-pro baseball team to watch. To enter Old Davis Park by the main entrance just behind home plate about 5:30 on a hot July afternoon was a thrill for a young boy of ten or an old man of eighty. It was the late 1940s and early 1950s. Television had not yet taken over our lives, and this was the place to be for the folks of the community.

The aroma of fresh popcorn, roasted peanuts, and hot dogs filled the air. You looked from the entrance just behind home plate at a freshly swept and lined infield. Long late-evening shadows of the stands stretched across the field. The players were playing catch, or "pepper," and getting ready for batting practice. A Sousa march like "Stars and Stripes Forever" would be playing softly over the PA system.

Batting practice would start, and hearing the crack of the ball against the bat and echoing several times off the old wood outfield fence was music in itself. The sound of the ball hitting the catcher's mitt was like a gunshot. After the old wooden fence was taken down some years later and replaced with a chain-link one, the magic of that echo was lost.

Yes, it was an enchanted place where many in Belmont spent a great deal of their lives, either watching or participating in baseball, football, boxing, donkey softball, and about every other event you could imagine that would attract a crowd.

The Belmont High School Red Raiders played their football and baseball games there for decades, thrilling fans with their skills. Bands marched and played. Cheerleaders danced. Fans yelled as games were being played by determined athletes looking for that super play that would make them a hero for the day. Great college players and major leaguers were made there too. Dreams came true for some, and some met failure and disappointment, but a million memories are floating around that old park to this day.

Tragedy struck in the early 1970s. Fire destroyed the old wooden covered stands. It was said to be arson. The magic was gone. The old field is still there but is now surrounded with metal bleachers and a metal fence. It is not the same without the covered wood bleachers and the wooden fence.

It is pleasant to remember the dugouts and the coldest and best water in the whole town at the drinking fountains. The old dressing room was where all that entered the door had bumped his head at one time or another because he didn't duck.

No young boy who walked on that field during the baseball season when Jules Jenkins was in charge of its care in the late '40s and early '50s will ever forget the cussing he got if he dared step on that green grass by mistake.

If you grew up in that time, you are now old. Tell someone, your children or your grandchildren, before it is too late. If you did not, you can refer to what has been said here. All we got now are the memories. Share them if you can.

—*BB*

EPIGRAM #14

For a Successful Day, Do Some of the Following Each Day

Do something for someone else.
Do something creative.
Do something selfish.
Do something learned.
Have a good laugh.

—*BB*

STORY #3

NC People, Places & Other Tales

Teachers and Coaches Molding Lives
A Person I Owe: Mr. Hugh Whitley, English Teacher
College Bound and Didn't Know It

The time was December 1956. The place was Belmont High School, Belmont, North Carolina. Football season was past. I loved football and was an average but eager player. I had played a little baseball, which I liked as well. I was a "utility player." That means I could play a number of different positions with some skill but had not been able to break into the starting lineup. I was, however, often substituted to replace a number of players when pitchers were shifted or someone was hurt. This is good stuff, but I digress from the main story.

I was an average student. I passed and was not dumb, but I took only the courses as necessary to graduate from high school. I took no advanced math, science, or language courses that were supposed to prepare you for "higher education." I just wanted to graduate. I really liked school, sports, chorus, and dramatics. Going to college was never in my thinking for the future. There were some good reasons for this lack of ambition for a college degree. The biggest one was my mother was widowed and worked on the second shift at a cotton mill, so the income was the "just enough to get by" kind. We had food, lived in a mill house, and had decent clothes and all, but we had no savings;

charging this week's groceries and paying for last week's was a hand-to-mouth existence for my mother and me. Oh, I had some kind of pocket money jobs, but we were not of the mindset about going to college.

As I said, I was not on the college preparatory course of study, but English was required four years for everyone. I was not a good speller, but I liked to write. I was also pretty good at sentence structure, so I was doing pretty well, not at the top of my class but also not at the bottom.

Mr. Hugh Whitley was a great English teacher. He was also the director of both the junior and senior class plays. I was in both his junior and senior English classes and in both the junior and senior plays. He knew me pretty well.

Again, this was my senior year. Football season was over. There was a long, open, and windowed hall connecting the old high school building and a new wing. Mr. Whitley's room was in the new wing. One day, I was headed to his class going one direction and he was going to the office in the other.

He stopped me and asked, "Where are you going to college?"

Surprised and astonished, I replied, "Me, Mr. Whitley? Going to college?" This possibility had never entered my mind. I continued, "Mr. Whitley, my mother works in the cotton mill for thirty-five dollars a week. We don't have any money to send me to college, and besides, I am not prepared with the proper courses to get in to a college." I, at least, was smart enough to know that.

He looked me directly in the eyes and said, "You are going to college, Mr. Brown. You be at my house on Woodrow Avenue Saturday morning by 8:00 a.m. We are going to Catawba College in Salisbury to arrange getting you enrolled for next fall."

You could have knocked me over with a feather. What could I say to a direct order from Mr. Hugh Whitley, my English teacher?

This was the middle of the week. He did not mention it again to me. What could I do? Saturday morning, I showed up promptly at 7:45 a.m. We got in his car, and off we went to Catawba College in Salisbury, NC. I dared not ask a question. What would I say? Some miles down the road, Mr. Hugh Whitley began to talk to this unprepared senior from Belmont High School about how I would not be allowed to waste a good mind and how even though I was not prepared with the right studies, I was going to be able to work, borrow, and beg funds to go. I just listened without comment.

We arrived at Catawba College in Salisbury around 9:30. They had classes on Saturday in those days, and there was plenty of activity on the campus. Catawba was an older church school and was physically like a college that you would see on TV or movies. It had an enrollment in those days of about a thousand or so students made up of campus and day students.

We parked the car and went straight into the administration building. Down the hall on the first floor were several offices. One had a sign on the door that read "Dean of Admissions." The door was open, so we walked in. Mr. Hugh Whitley spoke to the secretary, who smiled as if she had known Mr. Whitley for years, stood up, and motioned us to the door of the private office of the dean. We entered, and the dean stood up from behind the desk, walked around, extended his hand, and said, "Hugh, what a great pleasure to see you." They shook hands and exchanged conversation, indicating they knew each other very well. This was my first hint that Mr. Hugh Whitley, English teacher, was well known around Catawba College. I said nothing. I was scared to death.

Mr. Hugh Whitley finally turned to me and said, "Dean, this is Bobby Brown, and he needs to be a student at your college next fall."

The dean looked me up and down. He then said, "Well, Mr. Brown, why and when did you decide to come to Catawba College?" I could not answer. I looked at Mr. Hugh Whitley with a sideways glance and questioning eyes.

Mr. Hugh Whitley said, "Well, Dean, he is still thinking about it. He is one of my students. He is an average grade student, and his preparation in the courses of study for college has not been what it should be to gain entrance, but I will speak for him and tell you that with some remedial academic study, this young man will be a credit to our college. I am requesting that you make a special exception to allow a future student to fulfill his role in life, and that will require a college degree."

The dean said, and I quote, "Mr. Whitley, if you have the confidence in this young man that you have expressed, I have the same confidence in your recommendation, and I will see to it that an exception is made to the requirements for entrance to Catawba College for him. Mr. Brown, you have been recommended for entrance to this college by a most distinguished alumnus. We will both depend upon you not to make either of us look back and regret this decision."

That was it, and that is how I got in to that fine college in Salisbury, North Carolina. I owe a great debt to a person who saw in me something that prompted him to put his reputation on the line. I only attended Catawba College for one year. The reason was purely financial. In 1958, the general cost for attending Catawba College was about $1,200.00 per year. I was on my own financially. I could attend Appalachian State Teachers College in Boone for half that, or about $600.00 per year. I had no choice. Catawba College was a great school, but I just could not afford the price.

Transferring to Appalachian State Teachers College was a good move for me. I fit in and got along well. I was still an average student, but I believe Mr. Whitley would have been proud that this cotton mill hill kid had finally made the dean's list by my senior year.

I regret, because of circumstances beyond my control, that I never got to properly thank him in person for what he did for me, but I hope this little history may be some payback. Thank you, Mr. Hugh Whitley.

—BB

EPIGRAM #15

Life

Life might be compared to watching a freight train pass at a crossing. There is usually some finely drawn graffiti on some of the rail cars. You get only a moment to view someone's hard work and skill. In a flash, the train carries the scene away, never to be seen again. So it is with life. Now only a clouded memory remains.

—BB

STORY #4

NC People, Places & Other Tales

Molding Lives With A Pencil & An Old Royal Typewriter
A Person We All Owe: Belmont Sports Hall
Of Fame Inductee Dwight Frady

Dwight Frady is a person who we as fellow Belmont citizens were privileged to have known. Dwight is a lifelong award-winning sports writer, newspaperman, and a North Carolina citizen. Dwight is an honored recipient of the governor of North Carolina's Order of the Long Leaf Pine award. This is one the state's highest honors. Dwight changed many people's lives for the better with the stroke of his pen and the keys of his typewriter. He was a valued citizen who lived most of his life in Belmont, North Carolina.

I would like to share with you a "spoof and roasting" speech I made at a Belmont, NC, Honors Banquet held for Dwight Frady.

Ladies and gentlemen in this hall, it is a pleasure for me to recount to you some of the great moments in our honoree's life and career. Dwight has written stories on thousands of topics and as many or more people. He has beat out millions and millions of words on that old Royal typewriter of his about every subject you can imagine, but we all know his greatest love has been writing about and reporting on sports and the athletes who played the games. You name it, Dwight has written about it or taken a picture of most of it.

Let us look at the facts to support this statement. Dwight wanted to be a sports reporter and writer from the beginning, but as we all know, you can't just jump in and start at the top. The newspaper business is like most other businesses: most have to start at the bottom, proving themselves to be worthy, and then be promoted to more rewarding and important assignments.

So, Mr. Frady started out in the 1950s not as a sports writer but doing the jobs of a beginner with classified ads, obituaries, and general community news. But writing about sports was always on his mind, and every, and I mean every, opportunity he got, he would slip in a little sports news where it shouldn't have been. Let me share a few clips from the old papers of the 1950s in which Dwight was able to do just as I described.

Classified Ad, Dwight writes:
> June 8, 1953
> CAKE SALE
> Legionnaire wives to hold cake sale. American Legion Building. 2:00 to 6:00 pm Saturday. Sale location is just across from the Old Davis Park Baseball Field where Belmont's baseballers are playing for a Regional Championship at the same time. SO GO BUY A CAKE AND EAT BEHIND HOME PLATE.

Community News, Dwight writes:
> March 4, 1954
> BILLY GRAHAM IN TOWN
> Pastor Billy Graham to conduct services nightly this week at a local church. There could be a traffic problem as Belmont's basketball team hosts the Conference Basketball Tournament

that is being held nightly on the same street. THE REVIVAL STARTS AT 7:00 AND THE TOURNAMENT STARTS AT 8:00. LEAVE THE SERVICE A LITTLE BIT EARLY SO YOU WON'T BE LATE.

Community News, Dwight writes:

October 6, 1955

BELMONT HOSTS GOVERNOR

North Carolina's governor visited Belmont for the first time in history last night and spoke honoring a local fireman who saved two lives in a house fire. THIS EVENT WAS HELD JUST TWO BLOCKS FROM WHERE THE RAIDERS WERE PUTTING A POUNDING ON SHELBY. BELMONT SCORED FOUR TOUCHDOWNS. THE CROWD ROSE TO THEIR FEET, CHEERING AS THE FIREMAN ENTERED THE STANDS LATE IN THE FOURTH QUARTER. INCIDENTALLY, BELMONT'S SWIFT HALFBACK WAS RUNNING FOR A TOUCHDOWN AT THAT VERY SAME MOMENT.

So, as you can see by these writings, Dwight was always interested in writing about sports, even when he was not supposed to be doing so.

When Dwight began his career almost fifty years ago, he already had a unique style that captured the attention of his readers and sold newspapers from the very start. When he finally became a full-time sports writer, he didn't actually get paid for writing and covering the sports. No, he was on commission for the number of extra papers he sold.

This is how he worked it. He would come around to the teams and let the word slip that he was going to mention some names in the paper beforehand. Now, we didn't have copying machine available to us in those days, so he knew we would buy ten or maybe twenty copies each of an article with our name in it. We would probably be good for thirty if we ever were in a picture. The day the weekly paper would hit the streets, here would come Dwight in that old beat-up car of his loaded with extra papers to sell to the players. He liked making an extra buck.

In his sports articles, there was one great thing about Dwight that we as players always loved. He never tried to place the blame for bad play or a loss on anyone. The opposite would usually occur.

He always tried to make everyone look good. He was a genius at writing headlines for his stories that put forward the best side. I just happen to have a few of these old clippings, and I want to read a few to show you what I mean.

Sports News, Dwight writes:

September 15, 1956

RAIDERS HAVE BUSY NIGHT AT HOME

The Big Red had a busy time at Old Davis Park last night against a strong and determined Hickory High School team. Joe Lewis, Belmont's big lineman, ALMOST made two tackles. Fullback Buddy Eller JUST ABOUT made a touchdown, and tight end Wildman Williams WOULD HAVE CAUGHT A PASS had he not tripped over the rubber on the old pitcher's mound still in the infield on the 25-yard line. The punts of Belmont's fine punter, Doug Mauldin, would have gone at least 40 to 45 yards or more if they had not been blocked. Defensive back Kermit Williams looked great as he CAME REAL CLOSE TO INTERCEPTING TWO PASSES. And finally the score count could have been 30 to 7 if the Raiders had been able to score at least once.

Sports News, Dwight writes:
October 10, 1953
BIGGERSTAFF RUNS FOR TWO TOUCHDOWNS
Jim Biggerstaff, star tailback for the Belmont Red Raiders, ran for two touchdowns in their game against Shelby last night. UNFORTUNATELY, HE DID NOT MAKE EITHER ONE OF THEM.

Sports News, Dwight writes:
November 15, 1955
RAIDERS HAVE BEST LOOK OF THEIR SEASON
Belmont's Red Raiders football team had their BEST LOOK OF THE SEASON LAST NIGHT, EVEN THOUGH THEY LOST 30-0. THEY WERE WEARING THEIR NEW RED AND WHITE UNIFORMS FOR THE FIRST TIME.
Jimmy Hall, a major league player from Belmont, was a great baseball player. In his rookie year with the Minnesota Twins, he broke Major Leaguer and Hall of Fame inductee Ted William's Rookie Home Run Record. Several years earlier, Dwight wrote this story about Jimmy. He said he just wanted to be the first to break the news that Jimmy had gone to the big leagues before anyone else.

Sports News, Dwight writes:

> August 5, 1958
> JIMMY HALL BOUND FOR THE BIG LEAGUES
> Jimmy Hall, Belmont's super baseball talent, will be bound to the big leagues this weekend. He won two tickets in a WCGC RADIO CONTEST to see the Yankees play.

Sometimes, though, circumstances just forced Dwight to write and report player problems like the following article.

Sports News, Dwight writes:

> April 2, 1956
> BASEBALL COACH DISCIPLINES ACE PITCHER
> Belmont High School baseball coach John Painter had to discipline ace hurler Frank Traywick this week for wearing his hair and sideburns too long.
> (Note for the reader. So you can know. The funny part was that the ace hurler was mostly bald at the time except for long hair on the sides sticking out from under his baseball cap, which hid his baldhead. Frank, who was a guest at the time of the banquet, was now completely bald. Everyone enjoyed that, even Frank.)

Sports News, Dwight writes:

> 1990s
> COACH PHIL TATE STANDS HEAD AND SHOULDERS ABOVE OTHER SOUTHWEST CONFERENCE COACHES.
> (Note for reader: Coach Tate is about 5 ft. 6 in. tall.)

Following under the picture of the group of South West Football Conference the copy read, "Coach Phil Tate of Belmont stands head and shoulders above fellow coaches." (Because he is standing on a box.)

At the banquet, after the roasting, I said, "Dwight, there comes a time in one's life when all the truth just has to come out. Thanks for allowing us to have a little fun at your expense. Thank you for all your countless hours of work writing millions of words that made us look better than we really were and are. More importantly, you made us feel good about ourselves. You have always looked for and found the best in people to write about and not the worst. Thank you for what you have done for us all. You have not only recorded history, but you have also made history. You have well used your skills as a writer and your gift for seeing the best in others to share with the community. You are living proof that a man with a keen mind, a good heart, and an old, beat-up typewriter means more to the soul of the community than all the touchdowns, homeruns, and two pointers put together."

—BB

EPIGRAM #16

It is never too late to start something new.
—BB

STORY #5

NC People, Places & Stories

Teachers and Coaches Molding Lives
A Person I Owe: Belmont Sports Hall of
Fame Inductee Wrather Johnson
Taken from a Program Speech at a Belmont
Sports Hall of Fame Banquet

This man, Coach Wrather Johnson, had a great influence on the direction of my life. He was a coach at Belmont High during the 1940s and 1950s. He was known with affection as Mr. J, Coach J, or Mr. Johnson. He came to Belmont just after the war in 1946 as an assistant coach to head coach Gerald Cortner. Many at the banquet tonight either played for him or were taught by him.

After Coach Cortner became principal in 1953, Coach Johnson took over as head coach in 1954. He had had a short two-year head coaching career when he was named principal to the brand new New Hope Elementary School, where he served as principal for many years. I have always thought that to be an irreplaceable loss to the kids at the high school. What was obvious to all was that he had great affection for the students.

Coach Johnson tried to make every kid feel worthwhile and important in some way. He looked for the opportunity on the field to say something positive about even the weakest players on the team and lift them up in the eyes of the other players. He could chew on you with the same enthusiasm when you needed it too. He could motivate like no other coach I have ever known. He could talk to his team so that when he finished, he could have said, "Now, boys, we have to knock that wall over there down with our heads and without helmets." I do believe we would all have lined up and taken off the helmets and charged that wall.

Here are a few other things he would do that made him great. Each year after the football season, a banquet was held. This banquet, by the way, was a big affair for the team and the invited female guests. Coats and ties were needed for the players and party dresses for the female dates.

Mr. J had in hand before that banquet a list of the players, and matched with that player was who he knew was the player's steady girlfriend. He would query the player for the fact that he was indeed going to ask his girl to accompany him to the banquet. With those questions out of the way and marked on the team list, he would continue to approach the team members who were not "going steady" with a girl or did not yet have a date for the banquet. He also carried a list of many of the eligible girls neatly attached to the players' list. He would talk with each of the remaining players, some very shy, and ask if they had thought about who they might ask as a date to the banquet. "Jimmy, do you have a date as yet for the banquet?" If shy Jimmy replied that he did not, the next question would be, "Well, have you thought about someone you would like to ask?" If the answer was still no or a sideways headshake, Mr. Johnson would pull out the list and to show it shy Jimmy and say, "Do you see someone here that you would like to ask? Want me to ask her for you?" He worked very hard at this task because he knew how important this was to almost all the players to have someone to stand and sit with them at the banquet. I don't know that this effort was 100 percent successful, but it was an example of how much he cared for the happiness and well-being of the kids who were under his care.

Most all freshmen boys were in his health and physical education class. This was a real adventure. We went out to the field on Mondays, Wednesdays, and Fridays and had health classes on Tuesdays and Thursdays. You did not misbehave in Mr. J's class. He was in charge of your discipline, even when you were not in his class. He started off the physical education and health class with these words. "Is there anyone in the class who cannot remember one rule?" Again, Coach asked, "Is there anyone who is not smart enough to remember one rule?"

Some wise guy in the back spoke up and said, "Mr. Johnson, I don't think Brown can." That brought a roar of laughter and even a smile to Mr. Johnson's face.

Allowing the class of boys to settle down, Mr. Johnson walked to the blackboard, picked up a piece of chalk, and wrote across the board in huge letters, "DO RIGHT." He placed the chalk in the tray and began by reading those two words for us from the blackboard.

Mr. Johnson then said, "All of you boys are now fifteen, sixteen, and some seventeen years old. You all know the difference between what is right and what is wrong. There are unwritten rules of behavior here at Belmont High School. You know what they are without reading a list. I do most of the paddling here, so when you are sent to me for talking smart back to one of our nice, polite lady teachers and I get ready to tear your butt up with that paddle, don't say to me that you didn't know it was against the rules. When someone reports to me that you were smoking in the boys' bathroom and I am ready to tear your butt up with that paddle, don't tell me you didn't know it was against the rules. If you skip school, fight on the school grounds, or violate the other standards of gentlemanly behavior, the same rules still apply. Gentlemen," said Mr. J, "I get no pleasure out of using that paddle, but I will make darn sure neither do you. Any questions?" There were none.

Those of you here that played football for Coach J can remember the scouting reports he would give about the team we were up against for the coming week. He would describe how mean, fast, and tough they were. You would have thought we were up against the Washington Redskins or the Green Bay Packers. He would say that their running backs were so fast you couldn't even read the number on the jersey because they were blurred due to their speed. Someone with courage would ask, "Coach J, was he as fast as Doug Mauldin?" (Doug was an All-American High School halfback on our team).

Coach J would hike up his pants, gaze out the window for a few seconds, turn, and respond, "It would be a darn good race!"

When I became a sophomore and went out for football, everyone in those days who came out for the team did not get a "game uniform." I weighed about a hundred eighteen pounds soaking wet and had played two years of freshman football. I was trying out for the varsity team now. The day came for the issuing of the uniforms for the "traveling squad." I was the last kid in that gym that day with no game uniform, and it appeared that all thirty-six of the uniforms were gone. Coach Johnson went out the gym door. The five or six other boys who didn't "dress" left as well. I couldn't believe I had not made the "traveling squad."

I hung around as long as I had nerve, assuring myself that a great oversight had been made and was to be corrected. I finally stood up and started a slow walk out the gym door. The equipment room was just off the gym lobby. As I came out, Coach J was coming out of the equipment room with a red game jersey and a pair of pants about three sizes too big and threw them the few feet that separated us, and I caught them. He said, "Get your mama to sew up the back of the legs and in the waist so you can keep them up. Now get out of here."

I look back now and believe that he had not intended to dress me, but I looked too much like a lost puppy and he just could not turn me out. He made a decision that day that was more in the interest of the future of a scrawny fifteen-year-old kid than some other things. He broke, I think, a few of his own rules to hope something more important might happen.

Being on that team was the most important thing in my life at that time, and he recognized that fact. I shudder to think what direction my life might have taken had he not allowed me to be a part of that team.

Mr. Johnson was still a principal at New Hope Elementary School when I returned to Belmont in the early 1960s to teach and to coach freshman football, basketball, and baseball. Part of my job would be at his school several days a week while developing an elementary physical education program for the three Belmont district elementary schools. He would call me the day after my team would play the afternoon before and request that I be sure and come to his school so we could discuss the football game play by play. I think he was proud of me. I know that I was greatly influenced by Mr. Johnson not only in my work as a teacher and coach but also in the raising and teaching of my own children. For many years, when they would start out the door to go somewhere, they would say, "We know, Daddy, we know! THE DO RIGHT RULE!"

FOOTNOTE

After having read this little story, stop for a moment and think of someone who has had a great positive influence on your own life. If you have had someone, you are indeed fortunate. If they are still around, go tell them. If they are not, tell others about them.

—*BB*

EPIGRAM #17

A book is never too old if you haven't read it!

—*BB*

STORY #6

NC People, Places & Other Tales

Teachers & Coaches Molding Lives
Someone I Owe: Belmont Sports Hall of
Fame Inductee Everette "Ebb" C. Gantt

Belmont High School won its very first county football championship in the year 1939. "Ebb" Gantt was a member of that team. The yearbook pointed out that Gantt was one of the team's outstanding players. The team won nine out of ten games, scoring two hundred points to the opponents' forty. There is a story that Ebb was playing on the Belmont High varsity football team when he was in the fifth grade. He was big for his age and very competitive. After this last year of high school, he went on to play for the Belmont Abbey. Then, the war came along, and Ebb was drawn into the armed forces like many of his friends.

Ebb had started boxing long before he entered the armed services. He had an opportunity during the war to hone his fighting skills. He was good enough to win the Sacramento Air Command Fourth Air Force heavyweight boxing title.

After the war, he came back home to take his knowledge and talents to the field of play in baseball, football, and boxing. He began coaching Belmont baseball teams in the church league and produced some fine teams, at the same time teaching the skills of the games. There is a football on display in the Belmont

Sports Hall of Fame signed by all the players of the Red Raiders to Coach Ebb from 1946.

In 1946, just after the war, Gerald Cortner and Wrather Johnson came to Belmont High School to take over the athletic programs. Ebb Gantt joined them as an unpaid assistant and began to help build the foundations of high school sports in Belmont that we know today.

During this time, in the mid- to late 1940s and early 1950s, Ebb earned a living with the US post office as a mail carrier. He walked the route down Catawba Street through the mill villages of Belmont in the summer heat and the winter cold. He passed the fields where, when off work, he brought leadership and playing skills to the young boys of "Easten" and continued his volunteer coaching at the high school.

Just after the war, a young fighter already known as "One Punch" Guy Brown came to Ebb and asked if he would take him on as his trainer. Ebb hesitated at first. Guy Brown was tough and wild but said he was willing to submit to the demands of a training schedule that Ebb would demand if he were to work with Guy. This relationship proved two very important things: Ebb Gantt knew how to train and coach to help bring out the best in an athlete and Guy Brown recognized it. This leadership helped Guy Brown to become the professional Middle and Light Heavyweight Champion of the South in 1946 and later a Boxing Hall of Fame inductee.

Ebb continued his boxing and football coaching duties well into the mid-1950s. He produced championship teams and champion boxers. He then moved from direct coaching duties to the announcer's booth alongside Roscoe Helton to announce the Belmont High School football games. He next moved to the radio world, broadcasting games over the air for the Belmont radio station, WCGC.

Having the knowledge of the game's rules, skills, and players, Ebb Gantt found one of his greatest talents yet, which was bringing the excitement of competitive play to the ears of his listeners and making them feel as if they were in the arena and stands of the event. This illustrious radio career began in 1957, spanning three decades to bring him the highest honor a broadcaster can receive, the J. Robert Marlowe Merit Award for sportscasting in North Carolina. He served as president of the North Carolina Broadcasters Association in 1972. Ebb was inducted into the Belmont Sports Hall of Fame in the same year.

Where did I come into this Ebb Gantt world? Believe it or not, it was when I became his mail assistant. I was about ten years old. Ebb was the mailman with his walking route east on Catawba Street in Belmont and continuing to all the east part of town. I lived on Catawba. In the summer, I would join him. He would have the mail sorted so that he could hand me one side of the street's mail and he would take the other. After a while, I could have run the whole route by myself if necessary. It took all morning to deliver the route. Frankly, I was big help to him on those hot summer mornings. We would arrive back on Catawba Street and stop at the service station just across from my house. He would buy me a Pepsi Cola and hand me a crisp one-dollar bill for my help. Good money for a kid ten years of age. That was the time when Pepsis and Cokes sold for five cents.

I began to grow up, not very big but growing. Ebb coached the freshman football team. I played on his team in the eighth and ninth grades. I also boxed for a while on the Belmont Boys Club boxing team that he coached and led. He taught me that

I had to be in good physical shape, courageous, and determined when playing these sports. I was an average athlete, but what he helped put inside me were the important things for later in life. He helped guide a lot of kids into manhood with the right attitude about life. I am glad that I was one of them.

If Belmont ever had a true "Friend of Belmont Boys," it is no other than "Ebb" Gantt.

—BB, November 2012

EPIGRAM #18

Courage to Be Wrong

The real character of a person can be judged by how he can be on the losing side of the vote nine times out of ten and continue to voice his convictions. The tenth time may be when he is right, and his position could change the course of events for years to come.

—BB

STORY #7

NC People, Places & Other Tales

Angry With Eckerd's Drug: A Lesson Learned

Some years ago, my wife and I went shopping at a local chain drugstore. Now, it was a pretty good drug store and had most of what one would want to buy in that environment. It was late afternoon, just prior to supper, as I recall. My wife and I both had items to consider but on opposite sides of the store. As we entered, she went in one direction and I the other. After some fifteen or so minutes of shopping, we met back at the front checkout area to find that we were at the end of a long line with at least fifteen patrons waiting to check out. To make it worse, only one of the three checkout registers was open.

Well, that set you-know-who off because this was not the first time this had happened to me at this particular store. In a voice loud enough for all standing in the same long line to hear, I began to say things like "This is typical of this store. They want you to come in and buy their products but won't post employees at the checkouts, therefore wasting our valuable time. Where is the manager when you need him?"

Boy, that got my fellow customers in the line to start nodding their heads in agreement and murmuring things like "Yeah, right on brother, you tell 'em." Stuff like that.

"Well, I can tell you this," said I, "this will be my last trip to this sorry place." The other patrons in line, also mad about the delay, were almost clapping. This angry dude was letting them have it. All this time, my embarrassed wife kept pulling on my coat sleeve, trying to get me to shut up, but I would not.

Finally, after being in line for at least fifteen minutes, we were now down to about the fourth customers in line. I looked at my wife and said angrily, "What did you get?"

She replied, "Nothing. What did you get?"

I said, "Nothing." We looked at each other and then at the line of supporters looking at us. I slowly took her hand in mine and moved quietly around the checkout counter. Without looking back, we eased out the exit door and raced to the car.

I give a lesson here from me to you: before you start shooting off your mouth in anger, make sure you are not about to do something rude and stupid, particularly when you are with your wife.

—BB

EPIGRAM #19

Getting Old

The older I get, the less I know about more and more until I will know nothing about everything.

—BB

STORY #8

NC People, Places & Other Tales.

Mad at Santa Claus: A Fun Story with a Lesson

Santa Claus is the very last person in the world that an eight-year-old boy should be mad at, wouldn't you think? Particularly on Christmas Eve! Well, let me tell you about one who really was mad.

My mother's Watts family was large. There was Lacy, Lucy, Lorene, Pearl, Ruth, Sylvia, Walter, Alva, and Marshall. These were just Papa Watts's children, and they all had children. Christmas Eve was the big family gathering time of the year for the whole clan. We met at one of the abovenamed homes, everyone brought great food, and each one of Papa's girls had a special food or dessert that they were sure to bring. Kinfolks were overflowing out every door. It was great—playing with all the cousins, eating the rich food, and having lots of fun.

That was just minor to what was coming later in the evening. Santa Claus always dropped by for a visit on his way as he was delivering toys to kids all over the world at the same time. We didn't know how he could do it and visit as well, but he could. Santa Claus could do anything. He was magic. After we had eaten all the food our bodies would hold and waited for what seemed like hours and hours to all the believers, there would come a knock on the door, and when it was opened, there was Santa Claus. What a thrill! The real Santa at our Christmas party! Wow!

Santa would take a good chair provided quickly by one of the dads. Then, the children all lined up to sit on his lap, one by one. I was somewhere in the middle of the line of sometimes more than twenty-five or thirty kids. Finally, my turn came to sit on Santa's lap and tell him what I wanted for Christmas.

I climbed up on his lap, looked down at his hands, and suddenly a terrible feeling came over me. This person was not Santa. This was my older brother Guy. Guy was a professional fighter who was fifteen years my senior. I was very conscious of his fighter hand and knew every bend, cut, and finger. I thought, "They are just fooling me; there is no real Santa." I jumped off his lap and ran for the door. The uncles and aunts tried to console me, but I would not be consoled. I wanted to go home. I was mad, real mad!

Soon we were home. It was Christmas Eve, and I had just learned there was no Santa, "just someone pretending to be Santa," I said to myself. After what I thought was a very long time, I dropped off to sleep.

The next thing I heard was a knocking on the front door. Mother rose from her bed, turned on the lights and went to the front door. What I heard next was unbelievable. Mother said, "Why yes, Santa, he is right in the next room. Come on in. He's going to be real happy to see you."

I sat up in bed, and in walked Santa. He sat on the edge of the bed and began his conversation with me like this: "Bobby," he said, "I am really very sorry about your disappointment tonight at the Christmas party when you recognized your brother Guy in the Santa suit. You know it is very difficult for me to deliver all the children's toys and stop at all the parties to greet all the children, so I asked your brother to help me out at the party. I knew we could fool all of your cousins, but we knew you were too smart to be fooled. I am sorry to have made you unhappy, and that is why I stopped for a minute or so to speak to you about it."

My first question was "Where are your reindeer?"

Santa, being a very smart person, replied, "Why, they are just across the road in the baseball field. I do have to get on my way to deliver toys, and I will be back to deliver yours soon." Santa then patted my head and walked out the door to the sled and reindeer just across the road in the very dark ball field where there was no light.

What a night! Nobody dared tell me there was no Santa Claus for several more years or they were in for a fistfight. So, I have *never* gotten mad at Santa since, some sixty-seven years later.

—*BB*

EPIGRAM #20

Life's Races

One's whole life is made up of a series of races. Most start the race great and easily overcome the early hurdles when they are fresh and strong. The real test, however, is not at the BEGINNING. It is near the end of the race, the game, or the challenge that you are TESTED! The moment you are the MOST PHYSICALLY TIRED, THE MOST MENTALLY EXHAUSTED, THE MOMENT WHEN MANY LOSE THEIR WILL TO GO ON, THAT IS THE VERY MOMENT WHEN YOU BECOME A "WINNER" OR . . . a loser. WELL??????

—*BB*

STORY #9

NC People, Places & Other Tales

A Story: Your Call is Very Important to Us

How many of you just love to get this message when you call as a customer to a business of choice? "Thank you for calling XYZ Company. Your call is very important to us. If you are calling us about your back or late payment, dial 1. If you would like to make a payment, dial 2. If you would like information about clothes, dial 3, washing machines, dial 4, car repair, dial 5," and so on up through 10. "If you would like to speak customer representative about something, dial 0."

You shout, "Finally, I got it!"

Another computer-generated voice says, "All of our customer representatives are busy helping other customers. Your call will be answered in the order in which it was received. We are very busy on Monday, Tuesday, Wednesday, Thursday, and Friday. We are closed on Saturday and Sunday. Your expected wait time is approximately thirty minutes." Then comes the crappy music, loud and sorry!

Those of you who just love this customer-friendly, service-centered experience, raise your hand. Just as I thought: none, zip, zero. You know, customers are the ones with the money who want to buy things from the company that tells you right off that your call is very important, but they believe you have unlimited paid minutes on your cell phone, are retired, and have nothing better to do than to hang on to a line, waiting with steam coming from the top of your head.

A few questions come begging for answers here. Who does this wonderful, new computer-generated voice with a message benefit? Answer: not the customer! How many CEOs, sales executives, board members, or department managers have called their "customer service" line to try to reach a real human representative? Answer: My educated guess is very few. They probably all have a special line to the company's "real people."

WHY WOULD (capital letters means I am screaming) ANY SENSIBLE COMPANY SALES MANAGER, EXECUTIVE, OR CEO WANT A COMPUTER-GENERATED VOICE BETWEEN THEM AND THE CUSTOMER? (Remember, the customer is the person who has money and wants to buy the company's products and services.)

Don't answer. Forrest Gump has already told them, but they won't listen.

How many of you have been on hold half your day listening to terrible music when finally, a real voice says, "'Ello, my name is Olia. May I have your name, phone number, last four numbers of your Social Security card, credit card number, date of expiration, serial number of the product about which you are calling, and your wife's mother's maiden name? One moment please while I 'very fye' your account." Three to five minutes gets you back to Olia, who is often in a foreign country. "Thank you, Mr. Brown, and may I call you Bob?" (Might as well. We have been on the phone long enough to get intimate.) "Thank you, Bob. Now, how can I help you, Bob?"

"Yes, thanks. I wish to talk about the warranty on my new $1,000 computer that arrived broken."

"Ohhh, your computer! 'Verlie' sorry, Bob! I only know about CDs, DVDs, radio players, and iPods. I transfer you to another customer service rep that knows all about computer. Please hold, Bob." (Holding, holding, holding.) Then, a computer voice says, "Your call is very important to us. Your call will be answered in the order in which received. All computer service representatives are very busy helping other customers." (Real truth, they probably only have one customer rep.)

Now customer Bob is really getting mad!!!! Then, somewhere on the other side of the world, India, the Philippines, a long, long way from North Carolina, after using forty to sixty of his very precious cell minutes, Customer Bob, after a "verlie" long time, *gets cut off from his call.*

I make this observation: The "your call is very important to us" is a lie. If our calls to you and your company, Mr. CEO, Mr. Executive, and Mr. Sales Manager, are so important to you and your company, you would have a *real person* answering the phone and saying, "Good morning, this is the XYZ Company. How may we help you today? Service? Sure, let me connect you to that department." They would automatically start a new relationship with a new customer or continue a great relationship with an old customer.

The old sales motto "The customer's needs always come first" is never out of date.

—*BB*

EPIGRAM #21

Something About Dogs

Dogs come into our lives to teach us about love. They depart to teach us about loss. A new dog never replaces an old dog. It merely expands the heart. If you have loved many dogs, your heart is very big.

—*Unknown*

EPIGRAM #22

If you pick up a starving dog and make him prosperous, he will not bite you. That is the principle difference between a dog and a man.

—*Mark Twain, The Tragedy of Pudd'nhead Wilson*

EPIGRAM #23

I have tried to adopt this little statement as a guide for my life: I hope to be as good a person as my dog thinks I am.

—*BB*

STORY #10

NC People, Places & Other Tales

Me and My Dog Need an Old Couch
A Chance Meeting Becomes a Love Affair

It was still dusky and dark outside on this early August morning as I walked to the road to retrieve the paper. I always get the paper for my wife, who rises a little later, and I lay it at her place at the breakfast table. It's a little thing to keep on the good side, if you know what I mean. When I turned to take it to the house, I looked across my lawn to my neighbor's driveway where he parks his old white and red pickup truck. The light was very dim, but I could have sworn that I was looking at a lynx cat sitting straight and erect just beside it. I walked slowly across the yard toward it, and here he came running toward me across the grass. I soon saw that it was not a cat at all but a little black puppy with a long nose, half-bent ears, white paws, and a small red collar around its neck. I was then at the edge of our adjoining yard. He stopped about twenty paces away, said, "Woof," turned, jumped up the three steps on my neighbor's front stoop, and sat down. My attention to the puppy was cut short with the thought that some neighbor's kid owned the dog that had just momentarily escaped. My friend arrived in his car, ready to pick me up for a day of volunteer carpentry work.

I turned quickly, took the paper into the house, and returned to the car, and away we went. My only thought further this morning about the subject was that I liked that dog's ears.

When I got home later that day, for some reason I still had that little dog on my mind. Just for conversation, as I was giving my wife a report on the day's activities, I mentioned seeing that puppy this morning, that I first thought it was a lynx cat, and how he had run across the yard wearing a red collar, said, "Woof," and turned to the steps of the neighbor's porch. I went on to say I thought it was a neighbor's, maybe, and was just out of the fence.

The next day, sometime just after lunch, I was sitting in my chair. My wife came down the hall and said to me, "I just saw that little dog with the red collar running up the street." For some reason I cannot explain, I got up from my chair, went to the refrigerator, got a bottle of water, a piece of baloney, and a plastic bowl, and headed to the garage, where I got into my 1930 Model A Ford, and up the road I went.

I didn't have to go far, just next door. Again I saw him just under the front of my neighbor's old red and white pickup truck. I stopped, got out with my water and baloney, walked toward the front of the truck, and said, "Thirsty, Buster?" Here he came as fast as his little legs would carry him. I put down the bowl and began filling it with water. I could see he had not had anything to drink for some time. As he drank, I began tearing the slice of baloney into small pieces. After his drink, I reached out with the baloney. He was famished. He looked to be about three or four months old. His curled tail began to wag and his whole body with it.

My wife came out the front door of our house, and "Buster" and I moved to meet her. The dog ran to her at the steps with his tail wagging his whole body.

I said, "Keep him here while I go secure the gated area of the backyard."

Gail said, "What are you doing that for? We can't keep this dog!"

"I know, I know," I said. "I am going to just fix a place to keep him in until we can locate his owner. He belongs to someone in the neighborhood, I am sure. He has gotten out of their house. It won't take long to find them. We can't just leave him to run loose and maybe get run over." I headed around the house to the backyard.

We had just fenced part of the yard so that my daughter Lauren could bring her two King Charles Cavalier Spaniels to visit. Hers are housedogs, but this fencing would allow them out the back for short periods of time off the leash when she came to visit.

I secured the two pieces of moveable fencing under the deck, got a bigger bowl for water, and headed back around the house. Gail was seated on the steps, and "Buster." I knew he was still hungry. I asked Gail to watch him so I could run up to the store and get a little food for him. If he were going to stay with us while we looked for his home, he would have to have something besides baloney. Off to the store I went. As I left, I could see him following Gail down the driveway to the fenced area in the back. After getting back home with the dog food, we found another metal pot that would serve as a food bowl. We fed him again. Boy, was he hungry. We then began to further prepare for his "overnight visit." We found a box and put several old towels inside. The garage can be closed, so it was a good secure place for him to stay.

Now that he had food and water, he wanted to play and we could get a really good look at him. He was black with white paws and a white neck, and on his underbelly was a white area in the shape of a heart. His tail curled in a complete circle, and his ears flopped just short of the tips. "He is a handsome dog," I thought. We spent the rest of the evening before bedtime petting and playing with him, my wife, Gail, reminding me that we had to get busy the next day and find this dog's owners. I agreed, and we all went to bed. We left "Buster" in the closed and cozy garage and went upstairs.

We did not hear a peep out of this tired little pup the whole night. I had pleasant thoughts about this little sixteen-pound visitor most of the night. I do believe he had me at the first "Woof."

The Search Begins

"Buster" greeted me early the next morning with the same excitement and enthusiasm he had on the first morning we met. I petted him and led him to the side door that went to the fenced yard, and he went straight out and found a convenient bush. I couldn't believe I had found no mess in the garage.

His bowl was soon filled with food, and he gobbled it down just like before. I had found a little rubber toy in a box where the grandchildren kept things to play with when they visit. We played for a while, and then I invited him to go up the stairs to visit there. He was just as curious and excited as ever. I let him explore for a while and then took him outside. Gail, my wife, was not up, and I didn't want to awaken her just yet.

I sat down at the table and began to think how I was going to try and find his home. Our neighborhood is a closed community, with woods at the perimeter and only one entrance road. It is a community of about seventy-five houses. I decided that a little later in the morning, I would call a few neighbors and inquire if the dog might be theirs or a neighbor they might know. That would be a good starting point. I picked up the paper and began to read.

For some reason, I could not concentrate on the news of the day. I kept thinking about our little temporary visitor. Then, I began to remember our children, who were now all grown up and living lives of their own. We always had animals when they were growing up. We had everything almost that you could keep inside the city limits of our town. We had a series of dogs, cats, horses, ponies, a rooster, rabbits, gerbils, and more. They added a lot to our lives, and we enjoyed them. There are some great stories to be told too about how they enriched our family. However, once the kids were grown and gone and the last cat died, my wife and I vowed we would not have any more animals. We were free now to travel and do what we liked. We did not care for the responsibility that we once had with all the pets. That promise was made more than twenty years ago. No sir, no more pets for us.

My wife walked in and broke my thoughts. She said, "Well, where is that dog of yours this morning?"

"Well, darling, at this moment, he is in our fenced backyard playing with a rubber toy," I replied.

"Have you started thinking about how you plan to locate his owners?" she asked.

"As a matter of fact, I was just thinking about calling some of the neighbors on the other side of our community in a few minutes. You know, there has to be someone. This neighborhood is just too isolated for him to accidentally walk in. He's just a puppy."

Gail spoke further, "Well, you need to get busy. You know we can't keep that dog." She promptly got busy on the computer searching for notices about lost dogs.

The next day, our eleven-year-old twin granddaughters arrived. They were all excited about meeting "Buster," the lost dog we had told them about who had come to our house. "Buster" was excited about meeting them as well and showed it. We explained to them that we had not had any luck with our phone calls and computer searches for lost dogs as of yet. They talked and suggested that we make some flyers and put them at the mailboxes in the neighborhood. We got busy and soon had seventy-five lost dog flyers printed up on the computer. Around the neighborhood went Anna, Nico, Papa, and "Buster." We thought for sure someone would call us, but nothing happened.

"Buster" was still with us after the weekend ended. The relationship that began with a "woof" and a tail wag was now blooming into a full-blown love affair. I was getting nervous now that someone might really call and come to take him away. Even Gail was warming up. After some weeks, Gail and I decided to "lay claim" to our little sixteen-pound lost companion and give him a home.

He has been with us for over two years now. His full name is Buster Trouble Brown. Since I was old and had had a lot of experience with dogs, I thought I knew how to handle him. I would scold him severely for chewing up everything he could get his mouth on. I learned that when I fussed in a mean voice, it would break his heart. He understood every word. He would cower and pout. I would tell him I was sorry, and we would make up. We gradually got through that stage. I was learning and so was he. Gail was falling in love too. She did not want to at first, but she just could not help it. Buster Trouble had come into our lives and "adopted us" at an important time, and falling in love for us was wonderful.

Transitioning from Sleeping in the Garage

The first year of our relationship, Buster slept in his travel crate in the garage. The garage is heated, so it was very comfortable and cozy. We let him join us in the den in the evening. He had a doggie bed that was in front of the fireplace on which he would recline in all kinds of positions as he slept while we watched TV. Around 10:30, I would approach Buster on his bed and say, "Buster, it is time to go down outside to pee and then to the 'big bed' to sleep." Buster didn't move. He pretended he didn't hear me. I called again and said, "Look, Buster, I don't want to go outside either, but you have to go and get in your bed. You can't sleep up here." Finally, after about three times or more, he would roll over, get up slowly, and follow me down the stairs to do his business and get in the travel crate. I had to close the gate on the crate because he was still chewing up most things, even when he knew better. He just couldn't help himself.

One night, for whatever reason, we just took him out the front door for his nighttime business. I said to Gail, "Why don't we just let him stay on his bed in front of the fireplace tonight?" We did. Buster loved it. He has been sleeping on his bed in front of the fireplace ever since. If I am not up by 6:30, he comes to the bedroom to my side of the bed and says quietly, "Woof." I get up, and we start a new day.

Just a Little More

Buster Trouble is a very social dog. He likes people and he likes other dogs. We have a "doggie park" close to our home where there is a five-acre fenced area for dogs to play and romp. We go there regularly for the pure joy he experiences with other dogs. The dogs are all loose and on their own to choose other dogs for play. I, frankly, did not know that in this neutral ground dogs could be so social. He also has a girlfriend, a female dog just across the street. She weighs about seventy pounds, and Buster is about fifty. They love each other. We let them out to play with each other for thirty minutes or so many days. The wrestling is almost like a ballet. Each knows the other's moves, and they have a great social time. The front of our houses face each other across the street. Buster, behind our storm door, looks out, and Patches, on their driveway, looks across the road. They are like two kids waiting to have playtime with each other.

A Prize-Winning Dog

This past fall, we took Buster Trouble to the Plain Dog Show at our county park. Boy, did he look handsome! He had on his red collar, and I was decked out in my straw fedora and red suspenders. We entered him in two of the adult-owner categories: Best Behaved and Heinz 57 Mixed. Guess what? He got first place in both categories! Were we proud! That made us eligible for the Top Dog of the Day finals. At last, they called out to be judged for the "Top Dog of the Show." I looked around at the field. I looked down at Buster and said, "Buster, we got a chance here. You are the best behaved and most handsome dog here. We have really got a chance to be Top Dog." Just then, across the grass came a little old lady, pushing a walker with a very old little dog that had won the "Goldie Oldie" class.

I bet that dog was twenty years old and the lady was very old as well. Need I say more! Guess who was the "Top Dog of the

Show"? What more can I say about it? If I had been a judge, I probably would have given it to her too. Oh well, but we know, don't we, Buster?

What Buster Taught Me About My Wife

My wife, Gail, is a very particular person about hygiene and cleanliness. Eating and drinking after someone is taboo. Dishes and everything in the kitchen must be kept free of germs as she believes in the old adage "cleanliness is next to godliness." Buster and I like to go to Hardee's some mornings in my 1930 Model A Ford Tudor Sedan. Buster sits up in the front seat beside me and puts his nose out the window. We make a nice pair. All the girls at Hardee's know him by name, and they usually throw in a cold sausage biscuit for him.

One morning about a year ago, Buster and I took the three-mile trip to Hardee's to get some breakfast. This morning, we got the wonderful biscuits and gravy deal and headed home. Now, unlike some people, we feed Buster some snacks off the table. Small bites, you understand. When we eat, Buster has to eat. When we get biscuits and gravy, the gravy comes in a small Styrofoam cup and some is always left in the bottom. We let Buster lick the Styrofoam cup clean of what is left on the bottom. After I had put the gravy on my biscuit, I held down the little bowl and let him lick it clean. Gail then did the same with her Styrofoam bowl. Gail and I began to eat our biscuits and gravy from our bowls where we had transferred the gravy from the Styrofoam cup. I had just finished mine and looked over at Gail. I watched something that had I not seen it with my own eyes, I don't believe God could have convinced me that it happened. Gail took her bowl from which she had just eaten and in which some gravy was left in the bottom and handed it down for Buster to finish licking clean. My eyes went wide open. I could not believe what I saw my wife do. Gail looked at me and said meekly, "I am going to wash it out with some Clorox." My wife, whom I have known for some sixty-five years, had just taught me what real love for a dog could actually do to someone. What a wonderful and beautiful thing to learn about your lifetime partner that only Buster Trouble Brown could bring out. I am grateful to you, Buster, for what you taught me about my lovely wife.

**A Final Note Here About Being Adopted
by Buster Trouble Brown**
Buster Trouble Brown has been with us just over two years now and has brought such a wonderful feeling into our lives. He is the smartest dog I have ever known. He knows more English words than some people. He is also psychic. He can read your mind before you even say it. He even knows when the phone rings that it is from his girlfriend's master across the street calling for a playtime. He likes to sit with me in the porch swing with his head on my lap. I like it too. He is not allowed on our furniture. Maybe someday when we get "an old couch," he can do the same in the house. And it all started with a lost dog that just said, "Woof."

 —BB

EPIGRAM #24

Dogs and The Late-Night Pee

When I take my dog out to the yard for his late-night pee and I watch the way he smells everything in the whole yard, if I didn't know better, I would think that every animal from the Serengeti Plain in Africa had passed through since suppertime and he has to check them all out.

—BB

STORY #11

NC People, Places & Other Stories

Sir Winston of Churchill; or,
The Cat Really Did Come Back

Some years ago when our children were young, we lived on a street named Churchill Drive in our town of Gastonia, North Carolina. We owned dogs, cats, a rooster, a gerbil, a rabbit, and a couple of horses at one time or the other. My young son loved cats. There had been several kittens in his life who could not help but crawl under the car hood to a warm engine and then be attacked by the moving car when they didn't jump out in time. So there had been some sad times for the kids over these untimely accidents to the cats.

Our driveway's parking area at the house on Churchill Drive was at the end the drive and grew into a double-parking area for our two cars. You could walk from the car a few steps and be on a small back deck to the rear entry to the den. I could see when I pulled in the drive a little early this day that my wife's car was gone. I got out of my car and climbed the few steps to the deck as my wife was pulling in the drive to park beside my car. I waited for her to get out of her car. At about the same time, I saw my mother get out on the front passenger's side and my son exit from the rear door at the same time. I was surprised to see a grown cat exit with him.

"Well," I said, "what do we have here?"

My son, Brian, who was at the time about six years old, answered, "This is my new cat, and his name is Winston. We just got him from the pound. How do you like him?"

I replied, "You got a grown cat instead of a kitten? Where did he come from?"

Gail answered, "While we were looking for a kitten, we saw this cat. The pound attendant said a lady had brought him in earlier that day crying because she was moving and could not take him with her to the new place to which she was moving. As soon as Brian saw him, he went over and an immediate bonding took place."

"I want this cat," Brian said as he continued to rub and pet him.

Continuing, Gail said, "So, to make a long story short, here we are."

Here comes the wild part. On our street lived two dogs: a smart and feisty streetwise dachshund named Booger and a smart, larger Lab called Happy. In those days, there were no leash laws or what we had were loosely enforced, so some neighborhood dogs ran loose. Booger and Happy ruled this stretch of a six- or eight-house area on Churchill Drive. Our house was about in the middle of this dog kingdom. Most of the time, we had a yard full of kids, so the dogs were comfortable in ruling this domain completely. The rule for them was "We own this place and rule who comes in or out in the dog and cat world."

Just as we were about to continue the conversation about bringing home a grown cat, although he was really less than a year old, guess who came down the driveway to greet us? You got it—Booger and Happy. They took one look at the new cat, which I guess had been on the ground less than two minutes, and here went the dogs and cat, racing with a bang. Winston took off across the driveway with Booger and Happy right on his tail. Winston jumped the four-foot high chain-link fence in the backyard, and off through the neighborhood he went, out of sight. The dogs were trapped at the fence.

The wailing and the gnashing of the teeth began. I really felt so sorry for my son, Brian. His little heart was broken. His new cat was gone in a second. "Well"—I had the poor judgment to say it out loud—"that will be the last we will see of that cat. He is on his way back to the home where he used to live."

What could we do now? Nothing I could think of that would help. We made our way into the house with Booger and Happy strutting around as if to say, "Well, we did a good job with that."

We did get in the car shortly and cruised the neighborhood but with no luck in finding Winston.

It was not a happy time around our house for the next few days. Brian was inconsolable. I did not really know what to do. Looked like there would be another trip to the pound to try adopting a kitten.

I am an early riser. The morning of the third day of the cat's disappearance, I was up at first light and out to get the paper. It was going to be a sunny and bright day. I came into the kitchen from the side door with the paper. For some reason, I walked into the den, looked out the glass door window to the deck, and then opened the door. Who was there looking up at me, greeting me with a meow? It was he who was soon to become Sir Winston of Churchill Street. He continued looking up as if to say, "Okay, why so surprised? What's for breakfast?"

As words to the old song say, "The cat came back, the cat came back, and we thought he was a goner but the cat came back, 'cause he couldn't stay away." Winston lived with us for sixteen more years and was a wonderful pet.

Sir Winston of Churchill Learns to Spell

Sir Winston had been living with us for several years. He was smart cat. He didn't brag or flaunt it, but he knew what was going on around the house. He had lots of freedom because he was an outside cat, but he visited inside a lot. By that I mean he slept in the storage room just outside the side door at the drive. Some animals lovers might say, "You made him sleep out in the cold storage room?" Listen, this storage room was a luxury apartment as far as cat houses go. He had his cat door, central heat (the gas hot water heater was right beside his bed), and the butler and maid delivered food twice a day (that was my wife or me). He had it made.

Every morning when I went out for the paper, Sir Winston came in and visited while the family got ready for work or school. When it was time for us to leave, we called Winston to follow us out the door. He stayed out during the day while we were gone. Remember Booger and Happy? The two dogs that owned the territory for a block, greeted Sir Winston when he first arrived, and ran him off in the first part of this story? When they realized that Sir Winston belonged to the place, they all three spent most of the day lying around in the yard together sleeping.

Now, let us get on with the story. Normally, we took Winston to the veterinarian several times a year for a checkup and shots. On the night before, Gail and I would loudly remind each other that Winston had to go to the vet's for a checkup the next morning. Winston would be lying in front of the fireplace or on the top of the back of the couch, "pretending to be sleeping."

The next morning, we would let Winston into the house as usual to hang with us until time to go to work and school. When we called that day for Winston to follow us out, he could not be found. We did not like to leave him in the house, but we would have no choice. He could not be found. He was in a closet, under a bed, or somewhere well hidden and would not make a sound. So, no planned visit to the vet took place.

We thought we would get smart the next time by changing our tactics. We began to spell in front of him the night before. One of us would say, "Remember, Winston has to go to the V-E-T-E-R-I-N-A-R-I-A-N," spelled out, in a quiet, soft voice. The next morning, the same thing happened. Sir Winston would come in, but when it was time to go and he was called, no Winston.

We tried to use hand signals—he understood that too. From then on, we said nothing out loud. We wrote it down. The next morning, we would call him to the door, offer a treat, reach down, pick him up, and put him in the car. It is very difficult for humans to outthink a smart cat.

—*BB*

EPIGRAM #25

My Wife's Rules For Me When I Am Off To Make A Speech

No cussing, no sex stories, no politics, no religion, no medicine talk, and no illness tales about old people. What is left to say?

—*BB*

STORY #12

NC People, Places & Other Tales

Super Chicken: A "Cocky" Rooster

As I have told you earlier in this book, we were like many families in the 1970s and 1980s and had a menagerie of animals. Here is another episode in that adventure.

My eldest daughter, Lauren, was in the eighth grade. It was sometime in the spring of the year. I got home from work one day while it was still daylight. As I drove in to park at the rear of the house, I saw Lauren, Shannon, and several of the neighbor kids gathered around a table in the backyard. I got out of the car and approached them to see what was going on.

What I saw was a white baby chicken, or, as we say around here in the South, a little "dibbie." I approached the children and said, "Well, what do we have here?"

Lauren spoke up quickly and replied, "Dad, this is a chick from the science class. We had about a dozen of them. We have been studying the effects of growth hormones. We put hormones on some of them and others we did not so that we could learn the effects of the growth of the chickens' red cones on their heads. See how big this cone is? He was in the hormone group."

"That sounds real good, Lauren, and I am sure it was interesting, but what is he doing now at our house?"

"Oh, Dad," said she, "they were going to send them back to the chick farm where they would be grown into chickens for the stores to sell. The teacher said if anyone wanted to take one home, we could. So I did. Isn't he cute?"

"Lauren," I said, "we live in a neighborhood surrounded by houses. We don't live on a farm."

"Dad, look how little he is! He won't be much trouble, and we can just keep him in the yard—you could build a cage for him to stay in at night. He would just have gone back to die if I had not brought him home."

How does a dad argue with his daughter when she brings life and death into the conversation? I just turned, went into the house, and tried to block out the coming events in my tired and weary mind.

The next day, I began the project of building our new member of the household a home. I constructed a cage about three feet wide and two feet high. I used chicken wire, of course, and soon had a nice place for Foghorn Leghorn (named after the chicken in the Walt Disney cartoons) to live at night. He was pretty tame. He would let the children pick him up, eat out of their hands, and sit on Lauren's shoulder. As far as roosters go, he was a pretty well behaved for a chicken.

Time marched on. Foghorn, as I called him, began to grow and soon was living the *Life of Riley*: hand fed, sitting on the kids' laps, and following them around the yard. Putting him to bed at this time was no trouble.

At my place of work, one of the delivery drivers owned, with his wife, a chicken farm. One day ,I just happened to be on the loading yard where he was preparing to leave with a modular home. I knew he was a chicken farmer, so I began to discuss with him our new family acquisition of Foghorn.

He said to me, "Brown, I am going to bring you some special feed for that chicken. We use it to feed our chickens. You want to see Foghorn grow and become a real healthy rooster? You feed him the food I am going to bring to you tomorrow."

The next day, Joe brought me a thirty-five- to fifty-pound sack of his "special chicken feed." Foghorn was now about three weeks or so old and weighed about one pound. We started on this new feed that evening when I got home. He loved it. He ate well, and boy, did he start to grow. In about thirty days, Foghorn had gained a lot of weight and was growing a big red comb. I never saw a creature grow so fast! It was not long before he had to bend over in his two-foot high cage because he had grown so tall. He was becoming "Super Chicken." My friend brought me more food.

As I have told you all earlier, we lived in a neighborhood with houses all around. Now, things happen with roosters as they began to grow. One of the things is they want to start showing off and doing what roosters do: crow. They start to try out this new skill and practice about 4:00 a.m. Get where I am about to take you? You got it! The rooster coop was not more than forty or fifty feet from our bedroom window and not more than one hundred feet from several of our closest neighbors.

I was up and out the back door at 4:00 in the morning. I tried to scare the rascal into not crowing. You know, this terrorizing of the chicken worked the first night. Proud of myself, I headed back to my bed. The next night at about the same time, Foghorn started again. This time, he was getting better at the crowing. Not so much cracking of the voice. Then, there was a full-fledged cock-a-doodle-do that was heard throughout the whole neighborhood. I was back in my bed and couldn't get back to sleep.

Shortly, my phone rang. It was 5:00 a.m. I picked it up with a grouchy "Hello?" There was silence on the other end of the phone. It was one of my neighbors, I guessed. I gave another "Hello?" but still no answer. *Click.* I heard the phone go dead. In a minute, the phone rang again. "Hello?" from me but no answer on the other end, just mad breathing and a hang-up.

If I had not been so mad at that rooster myself, I would have answered the silence on the other end of the phone with a "COCK-A-DOODLE-DO"!

That morning at work, I approached another friend of mine who lived on about a sixty-acre horse farm over in Mecklenburg. My children and I knew him well as he let them come over quite often to ride the horses. I told Clyde about the rooster and the problem I was having with Foghorn in our neighborhood. He said he would be glad to take him in to live with the horses, cats, and dogs that he owned.

I told my children what we would have to do. They were not happy to have to give Foghorn up, but they understood and were trusting that this was a great place for him to continue to grow up. They could visit, still have a "relationship" with him, and be assured that he was not going to wind up on someone's Sunday dinner table as the main course. And we all slept well in our neighborhood from that day and ever after.

Now, what about "Super Chicken" and his new home? Foghorn was in his element. He was on a farm and the biggest and cockiest two-legged creature on the place. Standing almost three feet tall in his bare feet and with three-inch spurs on his legs, he took over. There were a few hens there that fell first under his control. Then, he took command of the gaggle of geese down on the lakeside. Even the housedog moved out of the way when he came strutting close by. The only ones he could not push around were the horses and ponies. When someone came up in car to visit and he was close by, he would drop his wings, put on his fiercest look, and charge the car. He was truly "the cock of the walk."

This was to be the case for several years, but alas, most tyrants don't stay on top forever. One sad day, one of Clyde's friends arrived for a visit in a pickup truck. Riding in the truck bed of the truck were two big bird dogs. "Super Chicken" was on the driveway. When the truck came to a stop ,he charged the truck. I don't care how tough a rooster is, he was no match for two full-grown bird dogs. Off the truck they came. "Super Chicken" stood his ground, though. Maybe if it had been just one bird dog, he might have had a chance. Two against one made the battle short.

Clyde, the farm owner, was saddened at the loss. A few of the loyal hens attended the burial. None of the gaggle of geese felt so inclined. When we went over to visit, my kids would visit the burial site in a moment of silence.

Oh well, nobody stays on top all the time.

—*BB*

EPIGRAM #26

Why Old People Can't Remember Stuff

Their minds are somewhat like old computers: they have used up all their available gigabytes.

—*BB*

STORY #13

NC People, Places & Other Tales

What's in a Name? Could be Trouble

Growing up, I never thought about it much, but having a common name like Bobby Brown can cause a lot of problems. Over the years, I have learned that it can cause mix-ups and the possibility of some serious trouble. In my small hometown of Belmont, there were three with that name. I was the youngest. We were all pretty decent guys, so there were not any real problems that I can remember.

My first serious encounter over my name was just after I was married. I was a teacher and coach. I worked long hours and had little time at home except for weekends.

One of the weekends, I was in the yard raking leaves on a beautiful and sunny fall day. As I was working in the backyard, I looked up and saw a man coming through the gate. He did not have on a police uniform, but he was wearing a badge and carrying a gun strapped to his belt. He approached and said, "Are you Bobby Brown?"

I replied, "Yes, I am one of them."

He did not smile at that and said firmly, "I have a warrant for your arrest."

A little shocked but knowing that I was not guilty of any violation of the good laws of our community, I replied, "What is the warrant for?"

He continued, "Passing a bad check."

"And where was this bad check written?" I asked.

"Bessemer City," said the man with the gun and badge. I still did not know his name. He pulled a folded check from his pocket and showed it to me. The name on the line was Bobby Brown, but it was not my signature—I could tell that at a glance. He had been quite impolite by not giving his name.

"Well," I said, "Mr. Person-with-a-badge-and-a-gun-and-no-name, I would like to inform you that, to the best of my memory, I have never ever been to Bessemer City in my life."

He replied rather sharply, "You are going to have to come with me to Bessemer City to appear before the magistrate."

My temper began to rise. This was my only day off. I had no intention of traipsing off twenty miles to Bessemer City for something I knew nothing about. I was in my own backyard, and I planned to stand my ground.

"Mr. Deputy, that is not my signature on that check. There are two other Bobby Browns in this town. I will give you a phone book, and you can look up their names and go question them if you like. I doubt if either one of them is guilty of such a thing as you suggest, but you can check with them. Tell you what I will do: I will go the several blocks in my own car with you down to the Belmont Police Station on Main Street. We can review in their presence the signature on that check with my driver's license, and that should assure you that it is not mine."

The deputy looked frustrated. I will say this: if he had pulled that gun on me, I might have considered his demands. He stood silent for a moment, and we looked at each other. It was his move. He began to turn toward the gate, looked back, and said, "I am going to check these others, but I might be back."

What a relief! A name can cause trouble. I have not been subject to arrest anymore, but friends have called to make sure I was not the Bobby Brown in the local obituaries. Occasionally, when first introduced to some of my friends of color, a smile will come across their faces at the name of Bobby Brown because of the famous black singer. I just tell them to tell all their friends that they met Bobby Brown today. They enjoy sharing that little story. I tell them to say after the fun that it was just the poor white one.

—*BB*

EPIGRAM #27

A Man's Responsibility at a Wedding

Remember, you are just a prop. You should show up in the approved outfit and keep your mouth shut until the appointed time for your two-line speaking parts, which are "I do" and "I will." For a successful and long marriage, continue to say them when you are prompted for the rest of your life.

—*BB*

STORY #14

NC People, Places & Other Tales

A Lesson Just for Laughs: the Tooth Psychiatrist

A few years back, my wife and I traveled with about eight of our close friends to Daytona, Florida. Two of the couples had timeshare condos at the same resort. We loaded up and traveled to Daytona for a week of fun, sun, and leisure. We had a great time on the beach, touring the Daytona race track, and seeing and doing many other great things. Everyone was happy and full of cheer.

Something usually happens on one of these great trips to stir things up a little. On about the fourth day, I experienced an unfortunate event. Well, I thought it was unfortunate, but most all the others in the group thought it a bit humorous, and I became the center of much laughter and fun for them.

We all were at an age when things are not always physically perfect with our bodies. In my case, it had to do with dental crowns. Modern dentistry is a wonderful thing. One can lose a few teeth, but with the miracle of modern medicine, they can fix these defects with what is commonly referred to as a crown. Well, old what's-his-name here happened to have three crowns in the upper front that were neatly attached and all bonded together. I had possession of these wonderful and handsome false front teeth that had become a part of my being. I could smile, laugh, and run my mouth, and these teeth looked, felt, and worked just like my old real ones. I was a happy man until this afternoon cocktail hour in the late afternoon in Florida. While I was feasting on a cold drink, some hard nuts, and popcorn (you know already what I am about to say, don't you?), these beautiful three front teeth, all supposedly bonded to my upper jaw, suddenly, without warning, popped from their mooring and right into my open hand that I quickly put to my open mouth.

Horrified, I was now exposed, and what used to be my smiling, talkative self was a snaggletooth old man who could not bear to remove his hand from his mouth. Gasps, moans, and sympathy for me broke out as all my friends realized what had happened. This didn't last long as a few smiles began to come to the faces of my "male friends" as it soon became less of a tragedy and more of a comedy matter. It was time now for the kidding and laughter. Even the women joined in.

"What am I to do?" Here I was, eight hundred or more miles from my dentist, holding my front teeth in my hand. After a while, I had to resign myself to the fact that I would be in this condition until I could get back to North Carolina. Then, I had a flash idea. We were to head home on Friday. I would ask my dentist to agree to meet me at the office and, at least, temporarily glue these three crowns back on until a better fix could be made at a later appointment. I announced my plans to the group.

"Good idea, Brown" was the resounding reply among the giggles and snorts of subdued laughter.

I headed to the phone and called information for the number of my dentist, Dr. Duren, in Belmont, NC. Information replied politely, and I gave her my request. Shortly after, I got a number and made my call. The secretary answered, "Dr. Duren's office." I didn't recognize the voice as it was a little strange, but I said, "This is Bobby Brown, one of Dr. Duren's patients. I am in Florida, and I have broken off three front teeth crowns. We are leaving Friday to come home, and I will be there Saturday. I would like him to come to his office this Saturday morning to meet me and temporarily glue these three front teeth back in place." There was a quiet pause on the other end.

"Well," the lady said in a strange and unfamiliar accent, "Dr. Duren is currently with a patient, and I cannot disturb him."

"Look, you must be new. This is Bobby Brown. I have been coming to his office for over fifteen years. Just ask him if he will meet me Saturday morning."

"Sir," she said, "please call back in about one half hour. I will talk to him and give you a reply."

"Okay," I said, "one half hour." Gosh, I thought, what a time to get a new receptionist in his office.

Thirty minutes went by, and I called back. The polite strange voice says again, "Good morning, Dr. Duren's office."

"Good morning again," I said for the second time. "This is patient Bobby Brown calling back as you requested. Madam, did you speak to Dr. Duren as I requested about fixing my teeth on Saturday morning?" Another long pause. I interjected sharply with this question: "Madam, is this the office of Dr. Jerry Duren the dentist in Belmont, North Carolina?"

She replied tersely and with the foreign accent in a more exasperated tone, "No, this is the office of Dr. Duren the psychiatrist in Burlington, North Carolina.

I yelled, "Dr. Duren, psychiatrist in Burlington?!" When I said that out loud, all my friends in the room, who had been listening to the one-sided conversation with the receptionist, began to snicker. Those grew into loud guffaws, and then some of the guys started rolling in the floor when they really understood to whom I had been talking.

Without reply to the secretary on the phone, I slowly hung up as the laughter in the room continued. I could just hear this lady on the phone saying to the psychiatrist Dr. Duren. "Doc, I got a nut on the phone who says he is in Florida and his three front teeth have fallen out and he wants you to meet him on Saturday morning to glue them back in. What should I tell him?" You can imagine for yourself what his answer might have been. Some of my friends might soon have needed medical treatment themselves if they hadn't stopped rolling in the floor laughing. Soon I began to laugh too. The greatest jokes are the ones that are on yourself and you can laugh at too.

Oh well, all's well that ends well. I did get in touch with Dr. Duren the *dentist* from Belmont, NC, that day. He did agree to meet me on Saturday and temporally repair my damage. The Florida trip that we thought was to cost nearly nothing turned out to be quite expensive when all the teeth were properly attached again.

—*BB*

EPIGRAM #28

On Politics

Do not forget, everything is political. Government, marriage, friendship, and business—it all requires negotiations. If you are not prepared for a little give and take, you are not going to make it.

—*BB*

STORY #15

NC People, Places & Other Tales

Shark Fishing and Oceangoing Freighters Don't Mix

This is a real live story about real live people. Well, it could have been a real live story about dead people had things gone in a different direction. The time frame was sometime in the mid-1980s. The place was North Carolina in the mouth of the Cape Fear River where it enters into the Atlantic Ocean. Now that we have the setting, let us get on with this story.

My old friend and coaching companion from the 1960s, Dave Smith, was an adventurer. He should have been born in the 1700s or 1800s. He loved the out-of-doors. He loved deer hunting, duck hunting, ocean fishing, and alligator hunting, and he lived in just the right place to do most of those things. That was the small town of Whiteville, North Carolina.

This North Carolina town is about fifty miles from the Atlantic Ocean and the Intracoastal Waterway that runs almost the whole length of the Eastern Seaboard.

Every year along the south coast of North Carolina and the northern coast of South Carolina was held a shark fishing tournament. Shark fishermen from all up and down the East Coast would show up to participate. It may still be held to this day. It was about a three-day tournament, and the prize money was pretty good for those who could come in first, second, or third. It was for the biggest sharks that were landed and brought by the fishermen to be weighed in. The shark fishermen were in it for the competition, but there were scientific benefits as well. Professors and students from the coastal colleges would come for the study and dissection of the creatures. Nothing was wasted that could be used for food or study. Dr. Frank Schwartz of the University of North Carolina system led this work and shark study.

Dave Smith had a twenty-eight-foot boat that was suitable for ocean fishing and travel along the coast. It had painted on the bow a picture of a shark with its mouth wide open and teeth shining. You could recognize it a mile away. Dave was an experienced boater. He knew his way around the coast. He was as strong as Sampson, as brave as Daniel Boone, as smart in the woods as Davy Crockett, and as adventuresome as Lewis and Clark.

This Dave Smith was a risk-taking outdoorsman. Trouble followed him like a shadow. If you wanted some obstacles to overcome, some danger to scare the hell out of you, or some adventure that you would never forget, you just took off on some outdoor trip with Dave Smith. This is the recounting of just one of those adventures that I was privy to participate in.

Let us get one thing straight to start with: Shark fishing is a nasty, dirty, hot, and tiring business. The crew spends all day getting the boat, the gear, the bait, and so on ready for the two-day adventure. One of the worst jobs is preparing the bait to attract the sharks. You spend half a day on the boat in the backwaters and marsh inlets casting a net to catch these small fish that school in these backwaters. I think they are called shad. After catching buckets of them, they have to be chopped up into all the bad-smelling stuff of dead fish. The day you are set up to fish, you have to pour pots full of this chum over the water to attract the sharks to the food and smell. Anyway, I just want to let you know it is not easy work or in the least bit a pleasant part of getting ready to compete in fishing for the biggest shark in the ocean.

The first day of the shark tournament was a terribly windy August day. The reason I know it was bad was that even the great adventurer Dave Smith thought it was too rough to attempt the trip out of the waterway into the ocean. I am glad he made that decision because it kept me from looking like a scared landlubber if I had to stand up and say I was not going out and to let me off at the nearest dock.

Dave, the captain of the boat (he was captain because it was his boat), suggested that we go up the waterway to the mouth of the Cape Fear River to fish. He said he had heard that some good-sized sharks had been caught there. This would keep us out of the rough ocean but still give us an opportunity to not waste a whole day of the tournament not fishing. It had cost several hundred dollars to enter, and we were not rich enough that we could just throw money away. Besides, we wanted to bring in a first place trophy and win the tournament.

So, off we went to the waterway, and in about an hour, we arrived at the mouth of the Cape Fear River where it entered the ocean. This North Carolina river goes up toward the Port of Wilmington, North Carolina, several miles northward.

The wind was really blowing, even here, at gale force. I am a landlubber and was out of my element, but I tried to act like I had been doing this all my life. By the way, I don't think I have informed you that this was my very first shark tournament.

Dave, our captain, pointed the bow of the boat into the wind, which was strong out of the southwest and powered us toward the bank, just about fifteen yards from the shore. He instructed his son to grab the anchor, toss it over the bow into the shallow water. He told him to let out the anchor line for about fifty yards. The bow of the boat faced the shoreline directly into the teeth of the strong wind. I felt like we were sort of like a twenty-eight-foot kite on a string, but those twenty-eight feet were the length of our boat. We were now anchored, almost but not quite, just in the middle of the mouth of the Cape Fear River.

Dave began to give orders to his two sons to bait hooks and get lines in the water. Since I am a landlubber, I was mostly watching and hanging on to keep from getting blown off the boat.

It was a clear blue-sky day. That wind I spoke of was really howling, and the anchor rope was stretched tight. The boys were working to untangle some fishing lines in the floor of the boat. Dave joined them. I looked up the Cape Fear River and saw a small boat approaching. When it got a little closer, I saw a big sign on the boat that read "River Pilot." I watched and as they passed some fifty yards to our stern. The pilot of the boat waved with his hands in a motion for us to get over out of the channel. Dave was hard at work in the bottom of the boat on the tangled lines. I advised him of the hand signals of the river pilot.

Dave replied to me, "He can't make us get out of the river." Then, his attention was back to the tangled mess of fishing lines in the bottom of the boat. He was the captain of the boat—what did I know about it? A few more minutes went by, and we all were focused on the problem in the bottom of the boat.

Then, we all heard it: the loud steam horn of a ship! Looking up, I saw the biggest ship I have ever seen, an oceangoing cargo ship that looked to be about ten stories high. The pilot was blasting on the horn. We were right in the path of this giant ship going to sea. I realized there was no place for him to go and he was not going to stop and ground his ship in this channel for some stupid landlubbers who claimed to be fishermen.

Dave jumped to the switch as the freighter horn kept blasting. He started the grinding of the starter for the engine. It would not start. What were we to do? I told you that Dave Smith was a modern-day Sampson. He jumped to the bow of our boat, grabbed the anchor rope, and hand over hand started the slow movement against a strong headwind to get us out of the path of that freighter, which looked now like it was twenty stories high.

My heart was in my throat. The ship was less than one hundred yards away and we were still in part of its path. Dave continued his Herculean effort to hand walk that rope to move our tiny boat out of the path of that giant freighter.

When the vessel passed by our stern, I remember looking almost straight up at the sailors looking down over the rail at our little boat and its terrified passengers that had almost become driftwood. The freighter slipped past and on out into the ocean.

We all were silent for a while and realized that except for this strong and determined man, our captain, we might just be at the bottom of the Cape Fear River at this moment. We quietly packed up our gear, weighted anchor, and headed for home.

Iron Man Dave Smith was not a quitter. That night, in a howling wind, he, one of his sons, and his son's friend left the dock of a safe harbor to go out and anchor about three miles off the inlet in the ocean to continue their quest for the biggest shark of the tournament. Landlubber Brown stayed on shore, of course. I became a shark tournament coastal radio operator in touch with the crew of this twenty-eight-foot boat called *Wave Dancer* on a very stormy sea. I considered my land job an important part of keeping contact with the crew on board. Around three o'clock in the morning, they radioed that they had hooked a shark and were fighting to land him. It was almost like listening to an old radio show when I was a kid. I could see them straining against the fishing pole, each taking a turn with the pole when the other would tire. The reports were short and sketchy, but they kept me on the edge of my seat for the next couple hours. Then, the report came over the radio: "We got him," said one of the crew. I applauded.

We went to the boat landing up the coast to meet them. They had the shark pulled up out of the water and tied onto the side of the boat. Now you could see two sets of shark's teeth shining: the ones painted on the boat and the real ones of the now dead shark.

The shark weighed in at about one hundred sixty-five pounds, as best I remember. I still have the picture of all of us with that shark as he hung from the scales at weigh-in. I have admitted that I was not on the boat when it was caught, but I was part of the team. I helped chop up that nasty bait and served as the base radio operator. That took a lot of guts, and I am proud. I retired from shark fishing that year.

My very dear friend Dave Smith, adventurer, passed away several years ago. He is sorely missed.

—BB

EPIGRAM #29

College Students; or, Who Does What?

An old college friend once told me that a professor was discussing student and grades. He said, and I quote, "'A' students teach; 'B' students work for 'C' students."

—*BB*

STORY #16

NC People, Places & Other Tales

Your Real Age Is? A True Story Just for Fun

Several years ago when I was about seventy years old, a few of our Belmont Historical Society friends were gathered and the discussion turned to something about our age. Jack Page's wife, Gearl Dean, was present. The subject expanded to health and fitness. Gearl Dean brought to our attention that Jack, her husband, would turn seventy-five years of age in the next few weeks and he was planning to ride his bicycle on a seventy-five-mile charity benefit ride on his seventy-fifth birthday. We all were impressed that at seventy-five years, he was in the condition to do so. Gearl Dean further reported that Jack had gone to the website realage.com, and after answering the online questionnaire about his general health condition, the program calculated his real physical age at sixty-two years.

I was impressed with that information. Later that day, I went online to the realage.com website, put in my name and age of seventy years, and began to fill out the questionnaire. Now, I did not expect the grand results that my friend Jack Page had gotten but was excited to hear the news. I will have to admit that I have had a number of health issues over the years, including two heart bypasses in the 1970s and 1980s, but I felt myself to still be capable and kept an active physical lifestyle with exercise, walking, golf, and the like.

My wife, Gail, was coming down the stairs as the website replied, "Mr. Brown, thank you for taking the realage.com testing. You will receive an email shortly giving your real age based on the answers to the questionnaire you filled out with reference to your health history."

I shouted, "Gail, come on down. They are getting ready to send me information on my real age questionnaire!" Gail walked into the computer room just as the email came up. We both looked at the screen with curiosity. The email read, "Thank you, Mr. Brown, for participating in the realage.com questionnaire. We are pleased to inform you that after due calculations of your health history, we have calculated your real age to be ninety-two years."

Sometimes there are things that you just really don't want to know.

Just out of curiosity, about a year later, I took the same test again. There had actually been an improvement. This time, the calculations said that my real age was only ninety-one years old. Cheers for good news.

—*BB*

EPIGRAM #30

To do something successful, you must first have a "real want to."
—*BB*

STORY #17

NC People, Places & Other Tales

A Stone Age Heart Bypass Story: A Forty-Year Heart Bypass Survivor's Story as of September 2015

Working to Give Others Hope as a Mended Hearts Volunteer

Long before the cell phones, video games, Apple computers, Doppler radar, the World Wide Web, operational GPS, compact disc players, and Viagra, coronary bypass surgery was developed. In 1967, a doctor named Rene Favaloro performed the first successful bypass surgery in America at the Cleveland Clinic. A large percentage of today's current U.S. population was not even born in 1967.

In 1975, I had my first coronary bypass surgery. I was thirty-seven years old. I was diagnosed with heart disease several years before and put on medication. Severe chest pains woke me in the middle of a hot August night. Ignorance and a hard head prevented me from going to the hospital that night, leaving me with pain and an anxious wife. I drove to the doctor's office alone the next morning and was driven to the hospital by my doctor in his own car and admitted to Gaston Memorial Hospital. That night, I had more pain and was administered nitroglycerin. My doctor entered the room the next morning and gave me these depressing words, "We are sending you to Charlotte Memorial Hospital"—now Carolinas Medical Center—"and you will be under the care of the Sanger Clinic physicians. Either you have something they can fix or something they cannot." Not a very comforting statement for a young thirty-seven-year-old with a wife and three young children.

Once in the CMS and under the care of Dr. Robicsek and his team, I was soon to learn that I was in a long line. The Sanger Clinic had just three surgeons and several cardiologists. They would not let me go home. They said, "If you go, you might not make it back." I spent one week waiting for a cath and then another week for the coronary bypass surgery. All this was so new to me. I really had not heard of coronary bypass surgery. I remember that the catheterization lab was primitive with water pipes overhead; it was painful in the groin. I also remember the bypass operating room being very cold and the table hard, much like marble that reminded me of a grave slab. I was very frightened.

I woke up unable to speak with the ventilator in my throat, tubes in my side, sewn up with stitches in my chest, and about the full length of my leg stitched up like an American League baseball.

I stayed two more long weeks before being allowed to come home to a wife who was carrying a very heavy burden with a sick husband, three small children, and a full-time teaching job. She was tough and terrific. There was no caregiver support from the hospital in those days for my wife. Recovery was slow. We were not prepared for the depression that followed. Frankly, they did not know what the post-operation world of the families was like until some years had passed. Later, they became more proactive with the caregivers.

I went back to work, survived until 1985, another ten years to the month, and was put on the operating table again for a second triple coronary bypass surgery. In 1989, I had angioplasty. They did not have stents in those days. In 2009, a defibrillator/pacemaker was implanted to protect me as I had developed diminished heart function leading to congestive heart failure.

I am now a member of the Mended Hearts chapter at Gaston Memorial Hospital, calling on heart patients who are preparing to have or who have just had heart surgery.

My good friend and our Mended Hearts chapter president, Jake Gray, will often say jokingly when we are teamed together calling on these patients, "You see this guy? He was operated on so long ago, they were still using stone tools."

I am proud to wear my badge that says, "I AM A 40-YEAR SURVIVOR." I am not there to brag; I am there to give hope to those who are now facing the ordeal of these operations to show that there is life after this very serious operation.

I am thankful to my wonderful wife, family, and friends who have helped make these additional years of my life worth living.

I am grateful for the skilled and dedicated doctors and other medical professionals who have, through their hands and skills, given an extended and productive life to me and now also to thousands of other wonderful and needy people.

To all you survivors of bypass or other heart repairs, I wish you a long and productive life.

—BB, a forty-year Stone Age heart bypass survivor

PS: I would like to pass on something that I heard Dr. Robicsek say on the radio in an interview a couple of years after he helped perform my bypass operation. The interviewer on the program was talking to Dr. Robicsek about heart disease when, toward the end of the interview, he asked this question: "Doctor, what is the one best thing our listeners and I can do to avoid heart disease?"

Without hesitation, and it a strong Eastern European accent, he replied, "Well, if it were me, I would choose my parents very carefully!"

Getting Old

The older I get the less I know about more and more until I will eventually know nothing about everything.

—*BB*

NC People, Places & Other Tales

The True Meaning of a Skeleton Key

This story is about the skeleton key. If you don't know what a skeleton key is, I will tell you. This is a key that will fit a number of locks. Why am I writing about such an inanimate object? Well, the key is only the vehicle for the story. The story is really about people and their nature.

I grew up in a small textile town in the South. The community was made up of many mill villages surrounding the cotton mill that provided the work and the housing for the workers. When the mills were built in the early part of the 1900s, there had to be homes for the workers. The "mill houses" were all built about the same time, but they differed in the number of rooms in each. There were three-room houses, four-room houses, five-room houses, and some six-room houses. This would allow for the accommodation of different-sized families in the community. In the small town of Belmont, there were at least fourteen mills with village housing for the workers. A lot of things were common, like the windows, doors, chimneys, etc., but the *most* common thing for all was the door key. All the locks on the mill houses were exactly alike with the *same* skeleton key. Strange, you say? Yes, but we lived in a different time. Where I grew up in one of the villages, almost no one locked the doors to the house. I do not remember anyone saying someone stole something from their house when they were gone.

What a wonderful thing to be a part of a community that had such trust and respect for their neighbors. Everyone who lived there worked in the same mill because you could not live in that village unless someone (usually the husband), worked in that mill. Some families would have a husband, a wife, and several children all working in the mill. Now, that does not mean that there were not disagreements between neighbors, kids, wives, and husbands, but the respect for the other person's home was an important part of this living relationship.

How would you feel today if everyone in your neighborhood had a key to your house? Most of you would not be able to rest or sleep a minute. We should pray for such times again, but I do not believe that it will ever happen. We live in a different world today.

—*BB*

Life

A life is a beautiful thing.
—*BB*

NC People, Places & Other Tales

A Story Of Healing In Life And Death

My wife and I lost our only son to death several years ago. I write this story not only to remember my son and his life but also to make the point of how one can really continue to give to mankind, even in death. He was a talented doctor, a caring husband, a loving father of twin girls, and a person admired and loved by his friends. He loved music, played the guitar, and enjoyed a cold beer. He was funny, creative, and a joker with his male friends. He had determination. When he was young, he was a cross-country runner (he didn't really care for team sports), a body builder, and somewhat of a health freak about what he ate. He was very intelligent. Got all that from his mother.

He was trained as a family medicine specialist. Brian and his wife returned to our hometown of Gastonia, North Carolina, and he began his practice of medicine with Caromont Health, a large hospital, and expanded medical care facilities in the Carolinas. He remained in this practice for over ten years. Brian's office was just across the state line between North and South Carolina near Lake Wylie.

Of course, I am proud of all my children. We have two girls: our first is a journalist and teacher, and our second is a nurse trained in the cardiology field of medicine. Brian came along last. He became a physician.

In 2007, I was retired. A young building supply owner in Clover I know called me and asked me to come work with him and manage the expansion of his business in Clover. Since I was retired, I was flattered and agreed to do so. Brian's office was only a few miles from this business in Clover. I went to work dealing with the building of the new warehouses for the building supply. I hired contractors for the project. One of these contractors was a grading contractor from the local area and just a little younger than I. We became friends very quickly. We could joke and kid each other about things, and it became a delight to see him on almost a daily basis for some months. One week, his partner was on the job for several days but not Joe. I asked about him, and his partner said Joe had been sick and gone to the doctor but should be back in a few days.

Well, when he did get back, I was right after him, saying he had just been lying out so his brother would have to do all the work. He assured me that he had been really sick, but he had gone to the doctor, the doctor had diagnosed his problem and prescribed the right medicine, and he was up and about the next day.

"Who is your doctor?" I asked.

"Oh, Dr. Brown just down the road at Lake Wylie."

I gave no sign that this was my son. I asked, "How do you like him?"

Joe replied, "He is great! And he is the smartest doctor I have ever known. My wife loves him. I think she just makes up an excuse just to go see him."

I said quietly, "That's my son."

He laughed out loud and said, "Your son? Your son? They ain't no way that boy can be your son. You might have the same last name, but that is as far as that can possibly go! I can't believe that you would think I am dumb enough to fall for some lie like that."

"So, you don't think I could have a doctor for a son?" I said.

"No," he said. "I will never believe such a bald-faced lie as that."

I said, "Well, just come into the office for a minute and I will show you."

He followed me into the building, still showing the little smirk on his face as I lead the way to my little desk, over which I had a bulletin board. Right there was a snapshot of my twin grandchildren, Brian's wife, my wife, and Brian. Joe leaned forward and got his face about twenty-four inches from the picture. I watched as this look of incredulity came over his face. His eyes widened as he turned to look at me. I do believe at that very moment, respect for my person went up 25 percent. He said, "Well, I'll be damned, Brown, I didn't believe you had it in you."

Before we went back outside, I had to reach over and change my hat on the rack for a larger size.

Death comes as a shock to all when it is someone close in the family. Over the past ten-plus years, we have lost five family members. All have chosen, prior to their deaths, cremation as the method of disposal of their earthly remains. We have family gravesites in the local cemetery in our hometown of Belmont, NC. All the ashes of the family have been placed in a final resting place on these family sites. It has been my sad but honorable responsibility, along with the other male family members, to prepare these sites for this final internment of the ashes. The ashes are placed in a container that can be settled in the prepared spot in the ground that is about ten inches across and some twenty-four inches deep. A named foot marker identifies the spot where the ashes are placed.

The remains from an adult who has been cremated are somewhat weighty. That is, normally ten or more pounds. I have been surprised at the weight as they were handed to me. When the ashes of my son, Brian, were handed to me to lower into the prepared spot, I was startled as to how light the container was. How could this be? He was a large man, and this package should have been much heavier. Then, it dawned on me: My son was an organ donor. Upon his death, some organs had been harvested for possible use to save or improve some other person's life.

My thoughts were later expanded to understand that because of my son's death, some other person's life might be saved and serve to help someone to have life that was yet to be born. Our son, who was a healer in life, helped to save and extend life while he lived and continued to do so, even in death.

My wife, Gail, and I will never recover from his death, but we can and do rejoice in the thought that he may well be continuing his life's work into perpetuity.

—*BB*

A Made-Up Mind

"A made-up mind is like a made-up bed: it's smooth and slick till somebody sleeps in it again and wallows around in it all night. Then it's all to do over again."

—*Author Ferrol Sams, Epiphany, 1994*

NC People, Places & Other Tales

Monday's Child

It was a dark, rainy Sunday night that December 10, 1939. My mother was in labor with her first child. My parents were at home in their small four-room rental house in Belmont, North Carolina. The heat for the breezy little cottage was from a lone fireplace glowing with hot coals or the kerosene cook stove in the kitchen. You had to be real close to it to stay warm or be covered up in the bed. My dad was just twenty-one years of age and had no experience with the births of babies. He was apprehensive, but he knew that the doctor had to be fetched.

Their little house was about three blocks from the National Cotton Processing Mill. The rain had been coming down for some time, and the unpaved roads were rutted and deep in mud. He instructed Katie, my mother, that she would need to get up out of bed and lock the door behind him to keep it from blowing open in the strong wind. The lock consisted of a piece of wood with a nail in it so it could be turned and hold the door closed. He also instructed Katie that she would have to get back out of bed when he returned to let him in the house.

Daddy put on his coat, turned up his collar, and went out in the cold and rainy night. Up the dirt road he walked quickly, dodging as much of the mud as he could, to the cotton mill several blocks up the street. The mill was not operating because it was a Sunday night, but Daddy knew that the watchman would be there and there was a phone in the mill. Most people in 1939 did not have phones in the home. Daddy said he had never talked on a phone in his life before that night. He found the watchman, who led him to the phone. The watchman helped him find the number. He dialed the number, making his first ever telephone call to Dr. Pressley, asking him to come to their home to help his wife, Katie, who was having a baby. Dr. Pressley said he would come right away. Daddy thanked the watchman and ran the muddy road back home.

Dr. Pressley soon arrived in his car. In the small house, Dr. Pressley began the instructions to Daddy about filling pots, heating water, and such. Daddy went to the back porch to the spigot, the only source of water, and began filling the pots and taking them to the stove to be heated up.

I was my mother's firstborn. Mother probably weighed only about ninety pounds before she became pregnant. I weighed almost nine pounds, so I can imagine it was a long, hard labor.

Well, I arrived on December 11th. Everything was in order, so Dr. Pressley told my daddy he would just stay the rest of the night. If he went back home, he said, he would just get another call and have to go out again. He was very tired and needed to rest. He pulled out a rocking chair, edged close to the fire, leaned back, placed his feet up on the brick front of the fireplace, and fell right off to sleep.

My daddy said he was so thrilled that the doctor was going to stay the rest of the night, he almost shouted for joy. My uncle commented on this story by saying, "The only difference between your daddy and Paul Revere that night was that Paul had a horse."

—Gail Brown on her seventy-sixth birthday, December 11, 2015

EPIGRAM #34

How to Tell if You are Over Seventy Years Old

Drivers of cars will stop for you and motion you across the drive in the Walmart parking lot.

—BB

STORY #21

NC People, Places & Other Tales

Just a Note Here Inserted for the Following Story
Don't think your children are not paying attention to what you are saying and doing. The wonderful birthday gift from my daughter Shannon that you are about to read below will, I hope, change your point of view.

—BB

A Birthday Present From Shannon Brown Flowers

To My Daddy On The Momentous Occasion Of Your 70th Birthday

"Just a few of the many reasons I love you," says Shannon.

I love that you still carry a real handkerchief.

I loved it when you brought home my first "Partridge Family" album.

I love that you still have the same hairbrush for the last 30? 40? 50? years.

I love that you taught me how to shoot a pistol, a shotgun, and a rifle and taught me a healthy respect for firearms.

I love that you adore our mother and always say how beautiful she is and you mean it.

I love that you built your own pontoon boat and took us to spend the night on it.

I love the way you always say, "Don't let me forget to turn the grill off, I am burning the grease off of it."

I love that you let us bring Lady home to OUR house to let her have her puppies.

I love that you are a good and loyal friend.

I love that you always know that you can complete ANY project.

I love how you taught us to respect and value our grandparents.

I love that you can't spell, just like me.

I love that when it snowed, you trusted me enough to let me drive in it.

I love that you can play banjo and guitar and never really took lessons.

I love that you want our family history to be important.

I love that you are a great dancer.

I love that you know so much about computers when many people your age just don't take the time to learn.

I love that you taught me how to change the oil in the "Bug" (the 1971 Volkswagen).

I love that you can always remember a joke or story and tell it even better the third or fourth time.

I love that you had us cut the grass when we were young. You always made us feel we could do anything, even though we were girls.

I love your "Do Right" saying.

I love that you taught me to drive a stick shift.

I love that you quit chewing tobacco.

I love how you have always been involved at church.

I love how you (and Mom) always sent me "extra" cash in college.

I love that you built us that great A-frame playhouse.

I love that great swing we had in our yard until the new neighbors moved in next door.

I love that you tried to put up a swing for your grandchildren that was just as good or better (which it was).

I love that you made us have "leaf raking parties" but would let us make "stalls and paths" and play before we had to bag them up.

I love how you (and Mom) almost always let us keep any animal we brought home.

I love how you weren't disappointed in me when I failed my driving test the first time.

I love that you think it is ok to cry.

I love how you used to play the piano and I would run up and down the living room with Mom's scarves (especially to that Spanish-sounding song).

I love that you taught me the importance of making up your bed as soon as you get up.

I love that you treat my husband like your own son.

I love that you enjoy reading.

I love that when I wrecked Lisa's car before I got my license, you knew I already felt bad enough without punishing me.

I love that you still didn't get really mad when I backed into two different people after I got my license.

I love that you have started a second "career."

I love how you keep all your nails and screws in those old peanut butter jars by type and size.

I love that you drove us to school in middle school when we really could have walked.

I loved it when you called "the Wizard" at my birthday parties.

I love that you would always check my car out before I drove back to college.

I love that you taught me how to check the oil.

I loved it when, after your car was newly waxed and it was raining, you let me slide from the roof and down over the trunk over and over again.

I love how you let us ride in the back of pickup trucks when we were young.

I love how you have never given up on that little bridge down in the backyard, no matter how many times it washed away.

I love how you do "projects" when you come to visit.

I love your "just pick up ten things" rule when cleaning up the kitchen.

I love your "every man for himself" dinner saying.

I love that you want to make a difference in your community.

I love how when we had horses that you taught us the responsibility and commitment for taking care of such an animal.

I love that you taught me how to play golf. And before that took me along just to drive the cart.

I love how you "throw out advice" and act like you don't care if we take it or not.

And I love that there has never been a day that I didn't know how much you truly love us all!!!

Happy 70th birthday!!!!

—*Shannon Brown Flowers*

Thank you, Shannon, for one of life's greatest gifts: the love of your children.

—*BB*

EPIGRAM #35

When being addressed on a political issue by an associate with whom you disagree, your best reply is "That is a very interesting point of view." Then, move on.

—*BB*

STORY #22

NC People, Places & Other Tales

Old Man's Disease: A Treatment Offered

I just have to include this story in this little book of writings, wisdom, and wit. I was watching TV one morning just recently, and the news program showed a picture of a short elderly man in a coat and tie being awarded an important honor plaque by none other than the president of his country. Leaning slightly to one side on his cane, he was shown holding his plaque in the other hand, and there, collected around his ankles, was the total of his fallen-down pants. Here was a very sad situation for all. How does one pull up his pants with a cane in one hand and a presidential award in the other?

This brings me to the point of this little instructional story. I am now in the category of what we call "old men." Old men become susceptible to all manner of ailments simply because they are aged. One of the worst conditions that can be contracted by many old men is called "NO-ASS-AH-TOL." This is the condition that the poor old man mentioned above suffered. This condition occurs when gravity pulls the butt toward the ground. The stomach rounds out, therefore taking away any grip that the man's belt might have had to hold up the pants at the waist.

However, there is a simple cure for this, and many have found the treatment to be common and readily available from any Walmart store. The cure is called SUSPENDERS. They are additionally referred to as braces, parachute straps, etc.

I have noticed that this condition is now spreading to the younger generation of the male species. I hope a cure can be found for them as well.

—*BB*

Now it is Time for Some Poems

Poems can be great stories, and sometimes they rhyme. A poem can still be a poem even if it does not rhyme.

—*BB*

I wrote this poem in 1989 for some dear and loving friends, Jayne and Dave Smith, of Whiteville, NC. The tree is located at their summer cottage on the Intracoastal Waterway at Ocean Isle, NC. It is filled with knots, twists, and limbs that inspire one's imagination for seeing all sorts of creatures.

The Ancient Tree

I have some friends who are dear to me.
They have a home close by the sea,
And in their yard stand two great trees.
The whole year round, they hold their leaves.
Their ancient limbs reach to the skies,
Shading all those who come just by.

The live oak's bark is now wrinkled and grayed,
Like most old men who by the sea have stayed.
Now as I stare at these ancient trees,
I see some faces looking back at me.

My excitement grows with each new face.
Am I the first to find this place?

More and more, now plain I see
All sorts of creatures looking back at me.
From the shadows of late evening's light,
A great giant bird is set for flight.
And in its beak an eel is caught.
A fine supper here for him, I thought.

From up-stretched limbs two arms are made,
A face between, a monkey played.
And just below the monkey's chin,
I plainly see a lion's grin.
And to the left, I almost scream,
A skull comes on the ghastly scene!

Right above the skull just there,
An Indian's head I see, I swear!
Then to the right, a limb dips down,
Old man winter's face is found.
The wind sweeps through his gray-black hair,
Almost as if he were carved just there.

Away up high there can be found
A possum with its tail around.
Just in the smaller limbs below,
A moose's face and antlers show.
The moon is up, the shadows low—
Can I find more before I go?

This ancient tree is old, you see,
Many more years than you or me.
It stands alone by the restless sea,
And you know how being alone can be.
Yes, while watching now it's clear to me
God put them there for our company.
—*BB*

POEM #2

My great-uncle William A. Day wrote this poem in the late 1800s. It is one of the many poems and writings by "Uncle Billy." He joined his Confederate regiment at the age of eighteen and served for the duration of the war until he was captured in 1865. He was the talented writer of the book *A True History of Company I, 49th Regiment, North Carolina Troops*, originally published in 1893 and reprinted in 1997 as the ninth volume of the Army of Northern Virginia Series by Butternut and Blue.

This poem was found in its original handwritten form along with other poems and writings by Billy Day in the museum of history, Old Courthouse Building, Newton, NC. Uncle Billy is the brother to my great-grandmother Margaret Jane Day, wife of Simeon C. Brown.

This poem, if not remembered for its style, should be forever read for the feelings of both sadness and happiness that it reveals from a great time gone by in our past, a time when honorable men were pitted against each other in a cause both sides believed to be right. Reading these lines that were penned some thirty years after the war reveals the depth of feeling remaining in the hearts of the old men of that great struggle. Listen as he travels through the five years of the war with his old men in arms. I, for one, hold it as one of the most moving and beautiful poems I have read.

—*Bobby Brown, great-grandnephew, 1999*

The Old Veteran's Parade

Get my old knapsack, Mary
Get my uniform of gray
Get my battered helmet, Mary
For I will need them all today.
Get my canteen and my leggings
Hand me down my rusty gun
For I am going out parading
With the boys of sixty-one.

Never mind these bloodstains, Mary
Never mind that ragged hole
It was made there by a bullet
That was searching for my soul.
Just brush off the cobwebs, Mary
And get my bonnie flag of blue
For I am going out parading
With the boys of sixty-two.

These old clothes don't fit me, Mary
Like they did when I was young
Don't you remember how neatly
To my manly form they clung?
Never mind the sleeve that's empty
Let it dangle loose and free
For I am going out parading
With the boys of sixty-three.

Draw my sword belt tighter, Mary
Fix the strap beneath my chin
For I have grown old and threadbare
Like my uniform and thin.
But I reckon I'll pass muster
As I did in days of yore
For I am going out parading
With the boys of sixty-four.

Now I'm ready, kiss me, Mary
Kiss your old sweetheart good-bye
Brush away those wayward teardrops
Lord, I didn't think you'd cry.
I am not going forth to battle
Cheer up, Mary, sakes alive
I am just going out parading
With the boys of sixty-five.
      —*Uncle Billy Day, 1880*

POEM #3

This poem was written in the 1990s after a busy family Christmas.

'Tis the Day After Christmas

'Tis the day after Christmas
And all through the house
Not a creature is stirring,
Not even a mouse.

The kids are all gone,
And it's quiet as can be.
Nobody is here
But the little wife and me.

The stockings are empty.
The food is all gone.
The kitchen is clear.
We're singing a new song.

We had a great time
And so love our kids.
We'll not soon forget
All the fun things that we did!

But now it is quiet.
It's time for a nap.
No grandchildren running
To leap on our laps.

With Gail in her nightgown
And me in my soft cotton pants,
We are both settled down
Now that we have a chance.

What a great gift
These children are, dear.
But now isn't it nice
With just you and me here?

Yes, Christmas is nice
And it brings us great cheer,
But I don't think we could take it
More than this one time a year!
 —BB

POEM #4

Shannon, my middle daughter, wrote this poem to me from Clemson in the 1980s.

Shannon and Money for College

Oh Daddy dear, I hope you hear
Things are tight today.
Would you be so kind?
If you don't mind,
To send some loot my way?
   —*Shannon*

The poem that follows is my response.

Ode to My College Daughter:

Money Is Not Everything

Oh $hannon dear, I clearly hear
Your cry for loot today.
To the bank I go, with haste you know,
To $end some down your way.

These college days, I hear you $ay,
Are filled with $trife and labor,
But fun and games, both are the $ame
The things I think you favor.

So a word of advice I give you now
And I'm $ure that you will heed,
These money fund$ I now enclo$e
Buy only what you need.

$low down for now in party town.
Omit the trips you favor.
A book to read, some note$ to take
Are now the things to $avor.

A few $hort weeks, I'm here to $ay,
Is all that's left, you know.
$o open wide your nurse book$, dear,
And keep your checkbook closed.
    —BB

POEM #5

We all want to be successful, whether we are trying to achieve something at the age of fifteen or seventy-five. We also know how important timing is in many of the things we attempt to accomplish. Being at the right place at the right time or being at the wrong place can make all the difference. Following is a little poem that points out just what I am saying.

Bad Timin':

One of Life's Lessons

I was stopped one morning on the interstate
In a broken-down car and running real late.
While waiting there for help to arrive,
Two possums happened to catch my eye.

They both were stopped in the median grass,
Just seeming to wait for the other to pass.
Then they both moved off at the same slow pace,
Right directly across the interstate.

Yes, both moved off as if neither could wait.
Bad timin', you see, is what sealed their fate,
'Cause, sadly, the first tried crossing too early
And the second tried crossing too late.

Now we all have choices as we come and we go,
Trying to think fast or when to move slow,
To watch out for things coming from the left or the right,
And prepare for dangers with all of our might.

So a lesson here we can learn today
When deciding what to do or to say:
Success is not so much in seeing what's right
As is making sure the timin' is right.
    —*BB*

POEM #6

To Measure a Man

How do you measure a man on his life?
Do you look at the things that he's won?
Or do you look at all that he has acquired
And review all the things that he's done?

Oh, you could take all these things, I guess,
And tell a great deal about some,
But a simpler test could really be used:
Just look at what he has left "undone."
    —*BB, 1995*

POEM #7

The Coach's Reward:
A True Story that Happened in 1962

It was a week and a half into practice.
The team, well, they looked pretty tough.
Good players at most the positions,
A few others looked ragged and rough.

There was some good speed at the tailback,
The line wasn't turning out bad,
But this offense called for a fullback.
The team needed a good one real bad.

Now the kid moved to town just yesterday;
That's why he was late coming out.
Some said he could play fullback,
So the coach was anxious to find out.

Heck, he ran that kid all evening.
Boy, was his tongue hanging out.
He knew as soon as he saw him run
He could be the new fullback, no doubt.

The very first game of the season
Proved to the coach he was right.
The kid ran and bullied like a veteran—
Scored twenty-four points on the night.

The second game soon came and went,
All with the same results.
The kid was the spark of the offense,
Pounding defenders to pulps.

Then Monday, there came the team captain.
He knocked at the coach's room door.
"I've got bad news," said the captain.
"The kid ain't gonna play anymore."

The coach was in a quiet panic
When he met the kid in the hall.
"Is it true what the captain just told me?
You, kid, want to quit playing football?"

"Yes, it's true," said the kid to the coach
As he stood with his back to the wall.
"I've got other things to be doing,
Like buying a car and what all."

Now, the coach he talked and he pleaded,
To the kid's pride and his strength he appealed,
Yes, all of the kid's feelings he tested,
But the kid kept saying, "No deal!"

"Well, it looks like it's all over,"
Said the coach very sadly at last.
"Turn in your gear at the office
As soon as you get out of class."

Later, the coach went on down to practice,
His face full of sadness, no less;
To lose a good kid with potential
Was a blow, he had to confess.

The kid's hands were deep in his pockets
As the coach was turning about.
"I was just wondering," said the kid to the coach,
"If you might let me come on back out."

The coach he was thrilled and excited,
Of course, not letting it show this time.
"You can come on back out," said the coach,
"But tell me, just what made you change your mind?"

The kid looked around, then spoke with a sigh,
"I thought about what you had said.
I know it sounds strange, but I just couldn't quit
After you talked to me the way that you did."

Now, the story goes on to greater success;
The kid, he improved more and more.
For outstanding play his name shows today
On a valuable player award.

Now, time has moved on for the coach and the kid—
More things to be done and be said.
We'll never know who it did the most good
When the coach talked to the kid as he did.

Let's hope for a time in your coaching years
When you're about to lose a good kid
That you'll hear these words: "I just couldn't quit
After you talked to me the way that you did."
    —BB, 1993

POEM #8

The Player

Oh, the fans they called him A PLAYER,
And man, did he look tough.
He was big and broad,
Looked hard as nails.
His voice was deep and gruff.

They all called him A PLAYER,
And boy, was he ever fast.
He could cut and turn
And block and dart
And really catch a pass.

They all called him A PLAYER.
Oh, his uniform looked nice.
That red and white, his helmet shined,
Made all the girls look twice.

They all called him A PLAYER.
College letters in the mail.
Yes, he looked great to all the fans.
This dude could never fail.

Yes, he looked for all like A PLAYER.
Everyone gave him the "HEY, MAN" shout.
But deep inside, where no one saw,
A little something was left out.

In practice, a half block on a teammate,
A lazy cut on a slow moving back—
Oh, nothing that the coaches could see.
He was too good for something like that.

Yes, the fans all called him A PLAYER.
Then, the game was on the line
When they needed his best effort
To win the big one this time.

Oh, he tried and he moaned and he grunted,
But his efforts they didn't work out,
'Cause deep inside where it counted,
That little something was left out.

Now, they all may call you A PLAYER,
Your name they can sing and shout,
But you can never call yourself A PLAYER
If you leave that little something out.
　　—BB

POEM #9

The Unsung Hero

You didn't often hear his name announced
Or was it seldom seen in print.
He didn't get the shoulder rides
Or high fives every place he went.

No touchdown pass, no touchdown run
Ever stood beside his name
He blocked, tackled, and did his job
'Cause he just played the game.

He stood the heat, the cold, and the pain.
He never said, "I quit."
He learned his job; he did his best.
He lived to block and hit.

Oh, he would liked to have heard his number
Sometimes called out in great acclaim,
But this fell second upon his list
'Cause he just played the game.

No college letter came in the mail
And bid him join their team.
No top awards being given out
Would ever show his name.

He gave his best from deep inside.
He never sought the fame.
This tough old boy just did his work
'Cause he just played the game.

His time is passed; the years gone by.
With new names the roster fills.
Big plays are made; touchdowns are caught.
New heroes are born and cheered.

Yet there's still the one we won't forget
Who never sought the fame,
Just being there was quite enough
'Cause he just played the game.

> *—BB, an "Old Raider," Class of '57, presentation of the Unsung Hero Award on December 7, 2000, continuing to this date each year to 2016*

POEM #10

Hope

Hope is knowing that everything is going to work out.
Hope is the rising sun in the morning.
Hope brings no doubt.
Hope is something you wait and wish for.
Hope is having faith.
    —*Charlotte Flowers, Bob's granddaughter*

POEM #11

Ode

The smell of cookies fills this picture from baking cookie dough.
All you can hear is the loud toys yelling like little kids.
The smell of plastic from bright toys.
The happy smiles of two little girls
With skin as smooth as silk.
Two girls leaping with laughter.
Sweet eyes jumping from the camera.
The love of sisters filled with hugs.
The messy hair from playing all day.
The little fingernails painted with pink.
With round button noses.
With the same brown hair.
　　—Charlotte Flowers, Bob's granddaughter

POEM #12

Wolf Song

Silently stalking,
Shadow in the trees.
Head up,
Scenting the wind.
Suddenly, a mournful sound erupts
From the depths of the soul.
The call is answered;
Many more are near.
Yellow eyes gleaming.
Snow flying to give illusion
Of glimmering misty wings.
Huge paws pound to catch the prize.
With a mighty leap, the prey goes down.
The others come, thick-furred and gray,
In a short family gathering,
Singing their sorrowful, eternal songs
To the crystal orb of the moon . . .
    —Olivia Owen, Bob's granddaughter

POEM #13

Restless

Wild as the sea,
Slow as a snail.
Frozen in time,
Unable to focus . . .
Energetic exhaustion,
Euphoric rage.
Racehorse's power
With nowhere to run . . .
Sleep?
A butterfly,
Fleeting, flitting,
Then gone entirely . . .
Vanishing like mist.
Earth stands still.
The creative soul dies.
At wit's end,
Monotony is shattered
Like fragile glass . . .
I breathe again.
   —Olivia Owen, Bob's granddaughter

POEM #14

This is presented here as a poem, but these are really the words for a song I wrote a couple of years ago. I composed it to sing with the Bluegrass jamming and picking group with whom I like to participate and play my guitar. There are a few aspiring songwriters in the group, so I wanted to show off.

When I was a young boy, my home was very close to the river and the Southern Railway. We played at the river a lot, and I remember some old cabins that were along its banks and very near to the railroad tracks as well.

There were then steam locomotives running the rails and the steam whistle was a wonderful sound that cut through the night air. I used my imagination to create this little song.

I told my fellow players this song would be soon sung on the Grand Ole Opry in Nashville, TN. That drew a big laugh from the whole crowd. What they did not know was that I was going to Nashville to visit my daughter and her family and planned to go as a tourist to the old Ryman Auditorium in Nashville, get on the stage with the guitar, and sing a verse of this ballad for my picture taking. When I returned from my trip, I showed them my picture on the stage and harassed the other would-be writers to step up to the plate and top it. I then confessed as to how it happened to more grins and laughter.

I am putting it here so that when this book is published, I will then be able to truly say that I am a "published song writer."

—*BB*

River Bottoms

Well, I got me a little old house
Right by the riverside.
I like sitting on the front porch,
Just when the train runs by.
Got me a little brown horse
And a great big yellow dog.
Got a little pig in a pen out back;
Gonna grow him to a great big hog.

Chorus
Oh, the train runs through here late at night,
Whistling a mournful sound.
Oh, how I love it down here
When there's no one else around.
Down here so nice and quiet,
No bustle, no people, no bother.
Right here is where I like to be,
Here on the river bottom.

Sometimes I wish I had a girlfriend.
Sometimes I wish I had a wife.
At times I wish for a big fine car,
Sometimes for a better life.
But I guess I am a lot better off
With me and myself right here,
A little shade, a little quiet,
And sipping on a good cold beer.

Chorus

I never went to school that long,
Never had a fancy job,
Never traveled to a far off place,
Never saw a bank get robbed.
I don't have no color TV,
No fine and fancy clothes,
But I know 'bout this river down here.
What else is there to know?

Chorus
    —BB

Parting Words to the Reader

Some years ago, there was a radio program that played on the air from early morning until about 10:00 a.m. or so. They may still be on the air, but I am retired, so early morning radio is not on my schedule these days.

The show was called the *John Boy & Billy Show*. I often listened to them on my way to work. They were very funny and had lots of verbal skits and fictional characters with whom they carried on with great humor.

One of the skits was when John Boy and Billy would ring up their business manager, Morrie, to discuss how he was doing to promote their careers. The skit was always complaints from John Boy and Billy as to why the manager was not making this or that take place in the radio world and why nothing was happening. The manager was always full of humorous excuses and explanations of just what he was going to be doing soon that was going to make them syndicated radio stars all across America.

After two or three minutes of such talk and supposedly frustrated angry questions to the agency, Morrie, their agent, would abruptly end the conversation with this comment: "John Boy, Billy, got to run. Bigger name on the other line." John Boy or Billy would begin to protest. Just before the agent hung up, he would interrupt with this line: "John Boy, Billy, love you, mean it."

Something wonderful evolved for my children and grandchildren from those harmless little skits. I began to use that phrase when we would have goodbye conversations. I, at some time, told them where it came from. It has become ritual between members of our family when we are ending a visit, a phone conversation, an email, a letter, or a parting goodbye. "Love you, mean it" has become a beautiful part of our family communication.

—*BB*

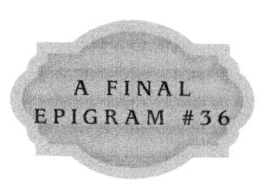

A FINAL
EPIGRAM #36

Just remember in life to be careful. All errors are not subject to correction.

—*BB*